MW00965136

HYMNS OF THE GURUS

HYMNS OF THE GURUS

Translated by
Khushwant Singh

VIKING

VIKING

Penguin Books India (P) Ltd., 11 Community Centre, Panchsheel Park, New Delhi 110 017, India

Penguin Books Ltd., 80 Strand, London WC2R 0RL, UK

Penguin Group Inc., 375 Hudson Street, New York, NY 10014, USA

Penguin Books Australia Ltd., 250 Camberwell Road, Camberwell, Victoria 3124, Australia

Penguin Books Canada Ltd., 10 Alcorn Avenue, Suite 300, Toronto, Ontario, M4V 3B2, Canada

Penguin Books (NZ) Ltd., Cnr Rosedale & Airborne Roads, Albany, Auckland, New Zealand

Penguin Books (South Africa) (Pty.) Ltd., 24, Sturdee Avenue, Rosebank 2196, South Africa

First published in Viking by Penguin Books India 2003

Typeset in Times_Norman by S.R. Enterprises, New Delhi
Printed at International Print O Pac Limited, Noida

CONTENTS

INTRODUCTION

The Sikh religion, a synthesis of Hinduism and Islam, is among the youngest of the Subcontinent's major religions. The word Sikh is derived from the Sanskrit *shishya* or the Pali *sikkha*, meaning disciple. The Sikhs are the disciples of their ten Gurus and worship the Granth Sahib (or Adi Granth), which is a compilation of hymns composed by the Gurus and other saints of India, both Hindus and Muslims. The Sikh Gurdwaras Act defines a Sikh as 'one who believes in the ten Gurus and the Granth Sahib', which definition, though not exhaustive, applies to a vast majority of the Sikhs.

A striking feature of the Sikh religion is its emphasis on prayer. The form of the prayer is usually the repetition of the name of God and the chanting of hymns in God's praise. Most of these hymns are contained in the Granth Sahib, and the remaining few, also included in rituals and prayers, are to be found in the *Dasam Granth* of the tenth and the last guru, Guru Gobind Singh. The hymns were composed by Hindu

Bhaktas and Muslim Sufis like Farid, Namdev and Kabir, and by the Gurus themselves (except the sixth, seventh and eighth Gurus, who did not write any) who were poets of great sensitivity. In this book I have put together a selection of hymns by the first five Gurus and the ninth and the tenth Gurus. Together, they communicate the essence of Sikhism.

***

The Sikh faith was founded by Nanak (1469–1539), the first guru of the Sikhs. He was born in a village about forty miles from Lahore (now in Pakistan). His parents were Hindus belonging to a Kshatriya subsect known as Bedis, i.e. 'those who know the Vedas'. Nanak was taught a little Arabic, Persian, some Sanskrit, Hindi and accounting. But his mind was never in his work. He spent his time meditating and seeking the company of wandering hermits. His parents found a wife for him. The couple had two sons. But Nanak soon lost interest in his family and once again reverted to meditating and wandering. A Muslim rebeck-player, Mardana, joined him, becoming his first disciple. Nanak began to compose hymns, Mardana set them to music, and the two began to organise community hymn-singing.

In the year 1499, when Nanak was thirty years old, he had a mystic experience. One morning while bathing in a stream, he disappeared under the water. According to his biographers, he found himself in the presence of God who spoke to him thus:

'Nanak, I am with thee. Through thee will my Name be magnified. Go into the world to pray and teach mankind how to pray. But be not sullied by the ways of the world. Let your life be one of praise of the Word (*Nam*), of charity (*dan*), ablution (*ishnan*), service (*seva*) and prayer (*simran*).'

Nanak was missing for three days and nights. When he came back, the first thing he said to the people who thronged to greet him was, 'There is no Hindu; there is no Mussalman.'

Nanak took to preaching. Accompanied by Mardana, he travelled extensively in India and abroad. He visited many holy cities of the Hindus and the Muslims, pointing out the folly of meaningless ritual and emphasising the common aspects of the two faiths. He spent his last years in a town called Kartarpur— meaning 'The abode of the Creator'—preaching and composing and singing hymns. He died in 1539 at the age of seventy. He was acclaimed by both the Hindus and the Muslims as the king of holy men.

Nanak's teaching reveals the influence of Hinduism and Islam. By the fifteenth century these religious systems had evolved some beliefs which had much in common. It was from the teachings of the Muslim Sufis, notably Sheikh Farid, and the Bhaktas, primarily Kabir, that Nanak drew his inspiration. From Islam, Nanak took its unqualified monotheism, rejection of idolatry and the caste system. From Hinduism, he borrowed the metaphysics of the *Upanishads* and the Gita. He elevated reality (*sat*) to the position of the One Supreme God. He accepted the theory of *karma* and transmigration of souls. The path he advocated was of bhakti, emphasising the worship of the name of God (*Nam-marga*). He rejected asceticism and propagated the *grihastha-dharma* (religion for the householder) and advocated the necessity of taking on a guru and keeping company with holy men (*saadh sangat*). Nanak also set great store by community hymn-singing (*kirtan*). He advised his followers to rise before dawn and listen to religious music, for he believed that in the stillness of the ambrosial hours (*amritvela*), one is best able to commune with God.

When Nanak died he left behind him a small community of Hindus and Muslims who described themselves as *Nanak-panthis*—followers of Nanak's way. They could at best be described as a group dissenting from both Hinduism and Islam. It was left to Nanak's successors to mould this group into a community with its own language and literature, religious beliefs and institutions, traditions and conventions.

Nanak was followed by nine other Gurus. Succession was not determined by the prevailing laws of inheritance, but with the object of finding a teacher most fit to safeguard and develop the spiritual legacy left by Nanak. It provided for two centuries a remarkable continuity in the functions of leadership, when one Guru succeeded the other 'as one lamp lights another'. Of the ten Gurus, the second, fourth, fifth, sixth and tenth were chiefly responsible for measures which fostered communal consciousness and welded the Sikhs into an independent community.

The second Guru, Angad (1504–52), was a disciple of Nanak and was chosen by him as his successor in preference to his own sons. The third Guru, Amar Das (1479–1574), was in similar fashion chosen from among the disciples. Angad developed the Gurmukhi script by combining the scripts current in northern India. He then proceeded to collect the writings of Nanak and added some of his own to the compilation. Angad established centres (*manjis*) for the propagation of Nanak's teachings. These *manjis* became meeting places for Sikhs, and later on temples (Gurdwaras) sprang up in their place. Amar Das consolidated Angad's work by increasing the number of *manjis* and introducing innovations to give Sikhism an identity distinct from Brahminical Hinduism. He preached against the seclusion of women, advocated monogamy, encouraged inter-caste alliances and forbade sati.

The fourth Guru, Ram Das (1534–81), laid the foundation of the temple at Amritsar. This temple was elevated into the Holy of Holies by his successor, Arjan (1563–1606), who also took definite steps towards organising the Sikh community. What Angad had started, he completed. He, along with his chief disciple Gurdas (1559–1637), continued the compilation started by the second Guru, and incorporated in it the writings of Hindu and Muslim saints. This became the Adi Granth or Granth Sahib, the holy scripture of the Sikhs. He was also responsible for the construction of temples at Taran Taran, Amritsar and Kartarpur, which became places of pilgrimage. Guru Arjan's organising activities attracted the notice of the Muslim rulers. He was arrested and, after considerable torture, executed at Lahore. He became the first and the most important martyr in Sikh history.

After the death of Arjan, Sikhism went through a transformation. It is said that the last message Arjan sent to his son and successor was: 'Let him sit fully armed on his throne and maintain an army to the best of his ability.' Hargobind (1606–45) accepted his father's advice and decided to train his followers in the art of defence. He girded himself with two swords, one signifying the spiritual and the other temporal leadership. By the time of his death, the Sikhs had already become a fighting force of considerable importance in the hill tracts and won several engagements against Hindu chieftains and local Muslim militia. Hargobind was followed by his grandson Har Rai (1630–61), a man of peace who adhered strictly to the routine of the life of prayer exhorted by Nanak; and Hari Krishen (1656–64), Har Rai's youngest son, who died of smallpox when barely eight years old.

The final transformation of the Sikhs into a militant sect came with the last of the ten Gurus, Gobind Singh. In the autumn of 1675, Gobind's father, the ninth Guru, Tegh Bahadur (1621–75), was summoned to Delhi by the Mughal Emperor Aurangzeb and ordered to accept conversion to Islam. The legend goes that he refused and volunteered to perform a miracle whereby the executioner's sword would fail to sever his head from his body. He wrote some words on a piece of paper and tied it round his neck with a thread like a charm. When he was decapitated the message on the paper was seen to read: *'Sirr diya, pur sirrar na diya'*—'I gave my head but not my faith'. It is also said that Tegh Bahadur repeated Arjan's advice to his son about arming the Sikhs.

Guru Gobind Singh (1666–1708) assumed the leadership of the Sikh community when he was only ten years of age. He spent the first few years in studying Persian, Sanskrit and the Hindu scriptures, and preparing himself for his mission. He realised that if his followers were to be saved from extinction, they had not only to be taught the use of arms but also convinced of the morality of the use of force. 'When all other means have failed, it is righteous to draw the sword,' he said. Even the conception of God became a militant one. He was timeless as death. His symbol was steel. Armed with these mental concepts, Gobind Singh set about 'training the sparrow to hunt the hawk and one man to fight a legion'.

On the Hindu New Year's Day in 1699, Gobind Singh assembled his followers and initiated five of them, known as *Punj Piyaras*, the Five Beloved, into a new fraternity which he named the Khalsa or 'the pure'. Of these five, one was a Kshatriya, and the other four belonged to the lower castes. They were made to drink out of the same bowl and given new names with the suffix 'Singh' (lion) attached to them. They swore to observe the 'Five K's', namely, to wear their hair and beard unshorn (*kesh*); to carry a comb in the hair (*kungha*); to wear a pair of shorts (*kuchha*); to wear a steel bangle on the right wrist (*kara*); and to carry a sword (*kirpan*). Gobind Singh further bade the initiates rid themselves of their family ties, their professions, their creed and ritual, and have no loyalties except to the new fraternity. After baptising the five, he had himself baptised by them. At the end of the ceremony, he hailed the five with the new greeting—'*Wah guru ji ka khalsa—Wah guru ji ki Fateh*': 'The Khalsa are the chosen of God—Victory be to our God.'

A significant step Gobind took was to declare the line of Gurus at an end. He did this while all his four sons were alive. He divided the concept of Guruship into three, viz. personal, religious and temporal. The first he said would end with him. The second would subsist for ever in the scriptures, and the Granth Sahib was henceforth to be considered as the symbolic representation of the ten Gurus. Temporal leadership he vested in the community, so that all decisions taken by the majority of a representative assembly became binding on the rest as if it were the order of the Guru himself (*gurumat*).

***

The Sikhs believe in the unity of God and equate God with truth. Although Sikh monotheism has an abstract quality, there is nothing vague about it. The preamble to the morning prayer, *Japji*, which is recited as an introduction to all religious ceremonial and is known as the *Mool Mantra*, the basic belief, states:

> There is one God.
> He is the supreme truth.
> He, the creator,
> Is without fear and without hate.
> He, the omnipresent,
> Pervades the universe.
> He is not born,
> Nor does He die to be born again.
>
> (Nanak)

There was a change of emphasis in the conception of God in the writing of the tenth Guru, Gobind Singh. To him, although God was still one, the aspect of timelessness and of the power to destroy was more important than the creative. He described God as *Akal Purukh* (timeless):

> Time is the only God,
> The primal and the final,
> The creator and the destroyer.
> How can words describe Him?

The attitude of the two Gurus which seems at first sight to be divergent is not really so. The basic factors in the conception of God were oneness and truth. Other attributes, such as omnipresence, omniscience, formlessness, timelessness, and the power to destroy evil, were complementary and also referred to frequently by Nanak. Guru Gobind gave them prominence by constant emphasis.

Although God has no form (*nirankar*) or substance and is beyond human comprehension, by righteous living one can invoke His grace. In the first verse of the morning prayer, Nanak said:

> Not by thought alone
> Can He be known,
> Tho' one think a hundred thousand times...
> How then shall Truth be known?

How the veil of false illusion torn?
O Nanak, thus runneth the writ divine:
The righteous path, let it be thine.

The Sikh emphasis on action as a means to salvation
is a departure from the predestination, and consequent
passiveness, of the Hindu belief. Nanak, who was fond
of using rural similes, wrote:

As a team of oxen are we driven
By the ploughman, our teacher.
By the furrows made are thus writ
Our actions—on the earth, our paper.
The sweat of labour is as beads
Falling by the ploughman as seeds sown,
We reap according to our measure
Some for ourselves to keep, some to others give.
O Nanak, this is the way to truly live.

Although Sikhism accepts the Hindu theory of *karma*
and life hereafter, it escapes the maze in which life,
death and rebirth go on, independent, as it were, of
human volition. The Sikh religion states categorically
that the first form given to life is the human ('Thou
has the body of man, now is thy turn to meet God'—
Arjan). Human actions determine the subsequent forms

of life to be assumed after death. It also believes that by righteous living and grace it is possible to escape the vicious circle of life and death and attain salvation.

The Sikh religion, believing as it does in the unity and formlessness of God, expressly forbids, in no uncertain terms, the worship of idols and emblems. Guru Nanak, while attending the evening service at a Hindu temple where a salver full of small oil lamps and incense was being waved in front of the idol, composed this verse:

> The firmament is Thy salver,
> The sun and moon Thy lamps,
> The galaxy of stars
> Are as pearls scattered.
> The woods of sandal are Thine incense,
> The forests Thy flowers,
> But what worship is this
> O Destroyer of Fear?

God being an abstraction, godliness is conceived as an attribute. The way of acquiring godliness or salvation is to obey the will of God. The means of ascertaining God's will are, as in other theological systems, unspecified and subject to human speculation.

They are largely rules of moral conduct which are the basis of human society. Sikhism advocates association with men of religion for guidance. Hence the importance of the guru or the teacher and institution of discipleship.

The Sikhs do not worship human beings as incarnations of God. The Sikh Gurus themselves insisted that they were human like other human beings and were on no account to be worshipped. Guru Nanak constantly referred to himself as the slave and servant of God. Guru Gobind Singh, who was the author of most of the Sikh practice and ritual, was conscious of the danger of having divinity imposed on him by his followers. He explained his mission in life:

> For though my thoughts were lost in prayer
> At the feet of Almighty God,
> I was ordained to establish a sect and lay down
>   its rules.
> But whosoever regards me as Lord
> Shall be damned and destroyed.
> I am—and of this let there be no doubt—
> I am but the slave of God, as other men are,
> A beholder of the wonders of creation.

Godliness being the aim of human endeavour, the lives and teachings of the Gurus are looked upon as aids towards its attainment. 'On meeting a true Guru,' said Nanak, 'doubt is dispelled and wanderings of the mind restrained.'

***

The compositions of the Gurus were always considered sacred by their followers. Guru Nanak said that in his hymns 'the True Guru manifested Himself, because they were composed at His orders and heard by Him'. The fourth Guru, Ram Das, said: 'Look upon the words of the True Guru as the supreme truth, for God and the Creator hath made him utter the words.' When Arjan formally installed the Granth Sahib in the Harimandir at Amritsar, he ordered his followers to treat it with the same reverence as they treated their gurus. By the time of Guru Gobind Singh, copies of the Granth had been installed in most Gurdwaras. Quite naturally, when he declared the line of succession of Gurus ended, he asked his followers to turn to the Granth for guidance and look upon it as the symbolic representation of the ten Gurus. (His own *Dasam Granth* is read with reverence but does not form part of rituals, except at the ceremony of baptism.)

The Granth Sahib contains the writings of the first five Gurus, the ninth Guru, and a couplet by Guru Gobind Singh. A large part of the book consists of the writings of Hindu and Muslim saints of the time, chiefly those of Kabir, who, like Nanak, was claimed by both Hindus and Muslims as their saint. The compositions of the bards who accompanied the different Gurus are also incorporated in the Granth.

The language used by the Sikh Gurus was Punjabi of the fifteenth and sixteenth centuries. Other writings are in old Hindi, Persian, Sanskrit, Gujarati, Marathi and other dialects of northern India. The entire work is set to measures of classical Indian music. The hymns are not arranged by authors or subject matter but divided into thirty-one ragas in which they are meant to be sung. Within the ragas, the compositions of the Gurus intermingle and are followed by those of the Bhaktas and the Sufis.

The Granth Sahib is the central object of Sikh worship and ritual. In all Gurdwaras, copies of the Granth are placed under a canopy. The book itself is draped in cloth, usually richly embroidered. It is opened with prayer and ceremonial each morning and similarly closed in the evening. Worshippers appear before it barefooted and with their heads covered. They make obeisance before it, and offerings of money or food are placed on the cloth draping the book. A ceremony of non-stop reading of the Granth Sahib by relays of worshippers, known as the *Akhand Path*, takes two days and nights and is performed on important religious festivals and private functions. Sikh children are named by being given a name beginning with the first letter appearing on the page at which the Granth may open. Sikh youths are baptised with recitation of prayers in front of the Granth. Sikh couples are married to the singing of hymns from the Granth, while they walk round it four times. On death, hymns are read aloud in the dying person's ear, and on cremation, they are chanted as the flames consume the body.

Despite all this, the Granth Sahib is not like an idol in a Hindu temple or a crucifix in a church. It is the source and not the object of prayer or worship. The Sikhs revere it because it contains the teachings of their Gurus. It is more a book of divine wisdom than the word of God.

GURU NANAK (1469-1539)
There are 974 hymns by Guru Nanak in the *Adi Granth*.

GURU NANAK (1469–1539)
There are 974 hymns by Guru Nanak in the Adi Granth.

JAPJI—THE MORNING PRAYER

(When he compiled the Adi Granth or Granth Sahib, the fifth Guru, Arjan Dev, gave Japji the first place in the sacred anthology. It remains the most important prayer of the Sikhs.)

There is One God.
He is the supreme truth.
He, the Creator,
Is without fear and without hate.
He, the Omnipresent,
Pervades the universe.
He is not born,
Nor does He die to be born again.
By His grace shalt thou worship Him.

Before time itself
There was truth.
When time began to run its course
He was the truth.
Even now, He is the truth
And evermore shall truth prevail.

1.

Not by thought alone
Can He be known,
Though one think
A hundred thousand times;
Not in solemn silence
Nor in deep meditation.
Though fasting yields an abundance of virtue
It cannot appease the hunger for truth.
No, by none of these,
Nor by a hundred thousand other devices,
Can God be reached.
How then shall the Truth be known?
How the veil of false illusion torn?
O Nanak, thus runneth the writ divine,
The righteous path—let it be thine.

2.

By Him are all forms created,
By Him infused with life and blessed,
By Him are some to excellence elated,
Others born lowly and depressed.
By His writ some have pleasure, others pain;
By His grace some are saved,

Others doomed to die, relive, and die again.
His will encompasseth all, there be none beside.
O Nanak, he who knows, hath no ego and no pride.

3.

Who has the power to praise His might?
Who has the measure of His bounty?
Of His portents who has the sight?
Who can value His virtue, His deeds, His charity?
Who has the knowledge of His wisdom,
Of His deep, impenetrable thought?

How worship Him who creates life,
Then destroys,
And having destroyed doth recreate?
How worship Him who appeareth far
Yet is ever present and proximate?

There is no end to His description,
Though the speakers and their speeches be legion.

He the Giver ever giveth,
We who receive grow weary,
On His bounty humanity liveth
From primal age to posterity.

4.

God is the Master, God is Truth,
His name spelleth love divine,
His Creatures ever cry: 'O give, O give,'
He the bounteous doth never decline.
What then in offering shall we bring
That we may see His court above?
What then shall we say in speech
That hearing may evoke His love?
In the ambrosial hours of fragrant dawn
On truth and greatness ponder in meditation,
Though action determine how thou be born,
Through grace alone cometh salvation.

O Nanak, this need we know alone,
That God and Truth are two in one.

5.

He cannot be proved, for He is uncreated;
He is without matter, self-existent.
They that serve shall honoured be,
O Nanak, the Lord is most excellent.

Praise the Lord, hear them that do Him praise,
In your hearts His name be graven,
Sorrows from your soul erase

And make your hearts a joyous haven.

The Guru's word has the sage's wisdom,
The Guru's word is full of learning,
For though it be the Guru's word
God Himself speaks therein.

Thus run the words of the Guru:
'God is the destroyer, preserver and creator,
God is the Goddess too.
Words to describe are hard to find,
I would venture if I knew.'
This alone my teacher taught,
There is but one Lord of all creation,
Forget Him not.

6.

If it please the Lord
In holy waters would I bathe,
If it pleases Him not,
Worthless is that pilgrimage.

This is the law of all creation,
That nothing's gained save by action.
Thy mind, wherein buried lie
Precious stones, jewels, gems,
Shall opened be if thou but try

And hearken to the Guru's word.

This the Guru my teacher taught,
There is but one Lord of all creation,
Forget Him not.

7.

Were life's span extended to the four ages
And ten times more,
Were one known over the nine continents
Ever in humanity's fore,
Were one to achieve greatness
With a name noised over the earth,
If one found not favour with the Lord
What would it all be worth?
Among the worms be as vermin,
By sinners be accused of sin.

O Nanak, the Lord fills the vicious with virtue,
The virtuous maketh more true.
Knowest thou of any other
Who in turn could the Lord thus favour?

8.

By hearing the word
    Men achieve wisdom, saintliness, courage, and
        contentment.

By hearing the word
    Men learn of the earth, the power that
        supports it, and the firmament.

By hearing the word
    Men learn of the upper and nether
        regions, of islands and continents.

By hearing the word
    Men conquer fear of death and the elements.

O Nanak, the word hath such magic for the worshippers,
    Those that hear, death do not fear,
    Their sorrows end and sins disappear.

9.

By hearing the word
    Mortals are to godliness raised.
By hearing the word
    The foul-mouthed are filled with pious praise.
By hearing the word
    Are revealed the secrets of the body and of nature.

By hearing the word
>   Is acquired the wisdom of all the scriptures.

O Nanak, the word hath such magic for the worshippers,
>   Those that hear, death do not fear,
>   Their sorrows end and sins disappear.

10.

By hearing the word
>   One learns of truth, contentment, and is wise.
By hearing the word
>   The need for pilgrimages does not arise.
By hearing the word
>   The student achieves scholastic distinction.
By hearing the word
>   The mind is easily led to meditation.

O Nanak, the word hath such magic for the worshippers,
>   Those that hear, death do not fear,
>   Their sorrows end and sins disappear.

11.

By hearing the word
>   One sounds the depths of virtue's sea.

By hearing the word
    One acquires learning, holiness, and royalty.
By hearing the word
    The blind see and their paths are visible.
By hearing the word
    The fathomless becomes fordable.

O Nanak, the word hath such magic for the worshippers,
    Those that hear, death do not fear,
    Their sorrows end and sins disappear.

12.

The believer's bliss one cannot describe,
He who endeavours regrets in the end,
There is no paper, pen, nor any scribe
Who can the believer's state comprehend.

The name of the Lord is immaculate.
He who would know must have faith.

13.

The believer hath wisdom and understanding;
The believer hath knowledge of all the spheres;
The believer shall not stumble in ignorance,
Nor of death have any fears.

The name of the Lord is immaculate,
He who would know must have faith.

14.

The believer's way is of obstructions free;
The believer is honoured in the presence sublime;
The believer's path is not lost in futility,
For faith hath taught him law divine.

The name of the Lord is immaculate,
He who would know must have faith.

15.

The believer reaches the gate of salvation;
His kith and kin he also saves.
The believer beckons the congregation,
Their souls are saved from transmigration.

The name of the Lord is immaculate,
He who would know must have faith.

16.

Thus are chosen the leaders of men,
Thus honoured in God's estimation;

Though they grace the courts of kings,
Their minds are fixed in holy meditation.
Their words are weighed with reason,
They know that God's works are legion.

Law which like the fabled bull supports the earth
Is of compassion born;
Though it bind the world in harmony,
Its strands are thin and worn.
He who the truth would learn
Must know of the bull and the load it bore,
For there are worlds besides our own
And beyond them many more.
Who is it that bears these burdens?
What power bears him that beareth them?

Of creatures of diverse kinds and colours
The ever-flowing pen hath made record.
Can anyone write what it hath writ
Or say how great a task was it?
How describe His beauty and His might?
His bounty how estimate?
How speak of Him who with one word
Did the whole universe create,
And made a thousand rivers flow therein?

What might have I to praise Thy might?
I have not power to give it praise.

Whatever be Thy wish, I say Amen.
Mayst Thou endure, O Formless One.

17.

There is no count of those who pray,
Nor of those who Thee adore;
There is no count of those who worship,
Nor of those who by penance set store.
There is no count of those who read the holy books aloud
Nor of those who think of the world's sorrows and lament.
There is no count of sages immersed in thought and
    reason,
Nor of those who love humanity and are benevolent.
There is no count of warriors who match their strength
    with steel,
Nor of those who contemplate in peace and are silent.

What might have I to praise Thy might?
I have not power to give it praise.
Whatever be Thy wish, I say Amen.
Mayst Thou endure, O Formless One.

18.

There is no count of fools who will not see,
Nor of thieves who live by fraud,

There is no count of despots practising tyranny,
Nor of those whose hands are soiled with blood.
There is no count of those who sin and go free,
Nor of liars caught in the web of falsehood,
There is no count of the polluted who live on filth,
Nor of the evil-tongued weighed down with calumny.
Of such degradation, O Nanak, also think.

What might have I to praise Thy might?
I have not power to give it praise.
Whatever be Thy wish, I say Amen.
Mayst Thou endure, O Formless One.

19.

Though there is no count of Thy names and habitations,
Nor of Thy regions uncomprehended,
Yet many there have been with reason perverted
Who to Thy knowledge have pretended.
Though by words alone we give Thee name and praise,
And by words, reason, worship, and Thy virtue compute;
Though by words alone we write and speak
And by words our ties with Thee constitute;
The word does not its Creator bind,
What Thou ordainest we receive,
Thy creations magnify Thee,
Thy name in all places find.

What might have I to praise Thy might?
I have not power to give it praise.
Whatever be Thy wish, I say Amen.
Mayst Thou endure, O Formless One.

20.

As hands or feet besmirched with slime,
Water washes white;
As garments dark with grime
Rinsed with soap are made light;
So when sin soils the soul
Prayer alone shall make it whole.

Words do not the saint or sinner make,
Action alone is written in the book of fate,
What we sow that alone we take;
O Nanak, be saved or forever transmigrate.

21.

Pilgrimage, austerity, mercy, almsgiving, and charity
Bring merit, be it as little as the mustard seed;
But he who hears, believes, and cherishes the word,
An inner pilgrimage and cleansing is his meed.

All virtue is Thine, for I have none,

Virtue follows a good act done.
Blessed Thou the Creator, the Prayer, the Primal
Truth and beauty and longing eternal.
What was the time, what day of the week,
What the month, what season of the year,
When Thou didst create the earthly sphere?
The Pandit knows it not, nor is it writ in his Puran;
The Qadi knows it not, though he read and copy the
    Koran.
The Yogi knows not the date nor the day of the week,
He knows not the month or even the season.
Only Thou who made it all can speak,
For knowledge is Thine alone.

How then shall I know Thee, how describe, praise,
    and name?
O Nanak, many there be who pretend to know, each
    bolder in his claim.
All I say is: 'Great is the Lord, great His name;
What He ordains comes to be,'
O Nanak, he who sayeth more shall hereafter regret
    his stupidity.

22.

Numerous worlds there be in regions beyond the skies
    and below,

But the research-weary scholars say, we do not know.
The Hindu and the Muslim books are full of theories;
    the answer is but one.
If it could be writ, it would have been, but the writer
    thereof be none.
O Nanak, say but this, the Lord is great, in His knowledge
    He is alone.

23.

Worshippers who praise the Lord know not His
    greatness,
As rivers and rivulets that flow into the sea know not
    its vastness.

Mighty kings with domains vaster than the ocean,
With wealth piled high in a mountainous heap
Are less than the little ant
That the Lord's name in its heart doth keep.

24.

Infinite His goodness, and the ways of exaltation;
Infinite His creation and His benefaction;
Infinite the sights and sounds, infinite His great design;
Infinite its execution, infinite without confine.

Many there be that cried in pain to seek the end
    of all ending,
Their cries were all in vain, for the
    end is past understanding.
It is the end of which no one knoweth,
The more one says the more it groweth.
The Lord is of great eminence, exalted is His name.
He who would know His height, must in stature be
    the same.

He alone can His own greatness measure.
O Nanak, what He gives we must treasure.

25.

Of His bounty one cannot write too much,
He the great Giver desires not even a mustard seed;
Even the mighty beg at His door, and others such
Whose numbers can never be conceived.
There be those who receive but are self-indulgent,
Others who get but have no gratitude.
There be the foolish whose bellies are never filled,
Others whom hunger's pain doth ever torment.
All this comes to pass as Thou hast willed.
Thy will alone breaks mortal bonds,
No one else hath influence.
The fool who argues otherwise

Shall be smitten into silence.
The Lord knows our needs, and gives,
Few there be that count their blessings,
He who is granted gratitude and power to praise,
O Nanak, is the king of kings.

26.

His goodness cannot be priced or traded,
Nor His worshippers valued, nor their store;
Priceless too are dealers in the market sacred
With love and peace evermore.
Perfect His law and administration,
Precise His weights and measures;
Boundless His bounty and His omens,
Infinite mercy in His orders.
How priceless Thou art one cannot state,
Those who spoke are mute in adoration,
The readers of the scriptures expatiate,
Having read, are lost in learned conversation.
The great gods Brahma and Indra do Thee proclaim,
So do Krishna and his maidens fair;
Siva and the Saivites do Thee name.
The Buddhas Thou made, Thy name bear.
The demons and the demi-gods,
Men, brave men, seers, and the sainted,

Having discoursed and discussed
Have spoken and departed.
If Thou didst many more create
Not one could any more state,
For Thou art as great as is Thy pleasure.
O Nanak, Thou alone knowest Thy measure.
He who claims to know blasphemeth
And is the worst among the stupidest.

27.

Sodar—(Te Deum)

Where is the gate, where the mansion,
From whence Thou watchest all creation,
Where sounds of musical melodies,
Of instruments playing, minstrels singing,
Are joined in divine harmony?
There the breezes blow, the waters run and the fires
    burn,
There Dharamraj, the King of death, sits in state;
There the recording angels Chitra and Gupta write
For Dharamraj to read and adjudicate.
There are the gods Isvara and Brahma,
The goddess Devi of divine grace;
There Indra sits on his celestial throne
And lesser gods, each in his place.

There ascetics in deep meditation,
Holy men in contemplation,
The pure of heart, the continent,
Men of peace and contentment,
Doughty warriors never yielding,
Thy praises are ever singing.
From age to age, the pandit and the sage
Do Thee exalt in their study and their writing.
There maidens fair, heart bewitching,
Who inhabit the earth, the upper and the lower regions,
Thy praises chant in their singing.
By the gems that Thou didst create,
In the sixty-eight places of pilgrimage,
Is Thy name exalted.
By warriors strong and brave in strife,
By the sources four from whence came life,
Of egg or womb, of sweet or seed,
Is Thy name magnified.
The regions of the earth, the heavens and the universe
That Thou didst make and dost sustain,
Sing to Thee and praise Thy name.
Only those Thou lovest and with whom Thou art pleased
Can give Thee praise and in Thy love be steeped.
Others too there must be who Thee acclaim,
I have no memory of knowing them
Nor of knowledge, O Nanak, make a claim.

He alone is the Master True, Lord of the word,
    ever the same,
He Who made creation is, shall be and shall ever remain;
He Who made things of diverse species, shapes, and
    hues,
Beholds that His handiwork His greatness proves.
What He wills He ordains,
To Him no one can an order give,
For He, O Nanak, is the King of Kings,
As He wills so we must live.

28.

As a beggar goes a-begging,
Bowl in one hand, staff in the other,
Rings in his ears, in ashes smothered,
So go thou forth in life.
With ear-rings made of contentment,
With modesty thy begging bowl,
Meditation the fabric of thy garment,
Knowledge of death thy cowl,
Let thy mind be chaste, virginal clean,
Faith the staff on which to lean.
Thou shalt then thy fancy humiliate,
With mind subdued, the world subjugate.

Hail! and to Thee be salutation.

Thou art primal, Thou art pure,
Without beginning, without termination,
In single form, forever endure.

29.

From the storehouse of compassion
Seek knowledge for thy food.
Let thy heartbeat be the call of the conch shell
Blown in gratitude.

He is the Lord, His is the will, His the creation,
He is the Master of destiny, of union and separation.

Hail! and to Thee be salutation.
Thou art primal, Thou art pure,
Without beginning, without termination,
In single form, forever endure.

30.

Maya, mythical goddess in wedlock divine,
Bore three gods accepted by all,
The creator of the world, the one who preserves,
And the one who adjudges its fall.
But it is God alone Whose will prevails
Others but their obedience render.
He sees and directs, but is by them unseen,

That of all is the greatest wonder.

Hail! and to Thee be salutation.
Thou art primal, Thou art pure,
Without beginning, without termination,
In single form, forever endure.

31.

He hath His prayer-mat in every region,
In every realm His store.
To human beings He doth apportion
Their share for once and evermore.
The Maker having made doth His own creation view.
O Nanak, He made truth itself, for He Himself is true.

Hail! and to Thee be salutation.
Thou art primal, Thou art pure,
Without beginning, without termination,
In single form, forever endure.

32.

Were I given a hundred thousand tongues instead of one
And the hundred thousand multiplied twenty-fold,
A hundred thousand times would I say, and say again,
The Lord of all the worlds is One.

That is the path that leads
These the steps that mount,
Ascend thus to the Lord's mansion
And with Him be joined in unison.
The sound of the songs of Heaven thrills
The like of us who crawl, but desire to fly.
O Nanak, His grace alone it is that fulfills,
The rest mere prattle, and a lie.

33.

Ye have no power to speak or in silence listen,
To grant or give away.
Ye have no power to live or die.
Ye have no power to acquire wealth and dominion,
To compel the mind to thought or reason,
To escape the world and fly.

He who hath the pride of power, let him try and see.
O Nanak, before the Lord there is no low or high degree.

34.

He Who made the night and day,
The days of the week and the seasons,
He Who made the breezes blow, the waters run
The fires and the lower regions,

Made the earth—the temple of Law.

He Who made creatures of diverse kinds
With a multitude of names,
Made this the Law—
By thought and deed be judged forsooth,
For God is true and dispenseth truth.
There the elect His court adorn,
And God Himself their actions honours;
There are sorted deeds that were done and bore fruit
From those that to action could never ripen.
This, O Nanak, shall hereafter happen.

35.

In the realm of justice there is law;
In the realm of knowledge there is reason.
Wherefore are the breezes, the waters and fire,
Gods that preserve and destroy, Krishnas and Sivas?
Wherefore are created forms, colours, attire,
Gods that create, the many Brahmas?

Here one strives to comprehend
The golden mount of knowledge ascend,
And learn as did the sage Dhruva.

Wherefore are the thunders and lightning,
The moons and suns,

The world and its regions?
Wherefore are the sages, seers, wise men,
Goddesses, false prophets, demons and demi-gods,
Wherefore are there jewels in the ocean?
How many forms of life there be,
How many tongues,
How many kings of proud ancestry?

Of these things many strive to know,
Many the slaves of reason.
Many there are, O Nanak, their numbers are legion.

36.

As in the realm of knowledge reason is triumphant,
And yields a myriad joys,
So in the realm of bliss is beauty resplendent.
There are fashioned forms of great loveliness;
Of them it is best to remain silent
Than hazard guesses and then repent.
There too are fashioned consciousness, understanding,
     mind, and reason,
The genius of the sage and seer, the power of
     men superhuman.

37.

In the realm of action, effort is supreme,
Nothing else prevails.
There dwell doughty warriors brave and strong,
With hearts full of godliness,
And celestial maidens of great loveliness
Who sing their praise.
They cannot die nor be beguiled
For God Himself in their hearts resides.
There too are congregations of holy men
Who rejoice, for the Lord in their midst presides.

In the realm of truth is the Formless One
Who, having created, watches His creation
And graces us with the blessed vision.
There are the lands, the earths and the spheres
Of whose description there is no limit;
There by a myriad forms are a myriad purposes fulfilled,
What He ordains is in them instilled.
What He beholds, thinks and contemplates,
O Nanak, is too hard to state.

38.

If thou must make a gold coin true
Let thy mint these rules pursue.

In the forge of continence
Let the goldsmith be a man of patience,
His tools be made of knowledge,
His anvil made of reason;
With the fear of God the bellows blow,
With prayer and austerity make the fire glow,
Pour the liquid in the mould of love,
Print the name of the Lord thereon,
And cool it in the holy waters.

For thus in the mint of Truth the word is coined,
Thus those who are graced are to work enjoined.
O Nanak, by His blessing have joy everlasting.

Slok (Epilogue)

Air, water, and earth,
Of these are we made.
Air like the Guru's word gives the breath of life
To the babe born to the great mother earth
Sired by the waters.
The day and night our nurses be
That watch us in our infancy.
In their laps we play,
The world is our playground.
Our acts right and wrong at Thy court
    shall come to judgment;
Some be seated near Thy seat, some ever kept distant.

The toils have ended of those that have worshipped
  Thee,
O Nanak, their faces are lit with joyful radiance—
  many others they set free.

* * *

panj nivajan vakht panj

There are five prayers
Each with a time and a name of its own.
First, truthfulness.
Second, to take only what is your due.
Third, goodwill towards all.
Fourth, pure intentions;
And praise of God, the fifth.
Let good acts be your creed: persevere with them;
Then proclaim you are a Muslim.
O Nanak, the more false the man
The more evil his power.

* * *

Moti ta mandir usraih ratani ta hoe jadao

Were I to live in a palace built of walls
Studded with pearls and rubies,
Fragrant with odours of musk and saffron
Smeared with agar and sandal

Lord, let not mine eyes be deceived by these
That I fail to recall Thy Name.

Without the Lord my soul would be burnt to cinders.
I asked my guru and now I know
There is no sanctuary but the Lord.

Were my floor embedded with diamonds and rubies,
On the floor a couch likewise with rubies inlaid
And on the couch a jewel-bedecked damsel
Sportive and wanton.
Lord, let not mine eyes be deceived by these
That I fail to recall Thy Name.
Were I endowed with powers to perform miracles,
To attract people by the gift of making gold;
Were I able to vanish and reappear at will
Thus strike awe in the hearts of the populace.
Lord, let not mine eyes be deceived by these
That I fail to recall Thy Name.

Were I a Sultan attended by retainers
With armies under my command and
My foot planted firmly upon my throne;

Were my word law, all revenues mine;
O Nanak, all this would be like thin air.
Lord, let not mine eyes be deceived by these
That I fail to recall Thy Name.

* * *

Kot kotee meri arja pavan peean apiao

Were I to live a million years in a cavern
Pierced neither by the sun nor the moon;
Too small to let me stretch myself,
Too small to sleep and dream;
Were my food and drink the air I breathed
(And I tried to assess Thy worth)
I would not know how great Thou art,
How then can I praise Thee?

He is the Truth, He is without form.
He is self-existent, His status is unique.
We hear of Him, then we speak of Him.
If He wills we have to know Him.
Were I to be slashed to shreds
Minced and ground to pulp
Fired in a furnace, with ashes mingled,
I would not know how great Thou art.

Were I a bird soaring through a hundred skies
Beyond the range of vision
Feeding on nothing, drinking nothing,
I would not know how great Thou art,
How then can I praise Thee?

O Nanak, had I a hundred thousand tons of paper
And filled the pages with essence of learning
Pen plying with the speed of wind, dipping in an
    inexhaustible inkwell,
Even so
I would not know how great Thou art,
How then can I praise Thee?

* * *

Lekhai bolan bolana lekhai khana khao

There is a limit to the amount we talk
And to the food we eat;
There is a limit to our wanderings
To the sights we see, to the sounds we hear;
There is a limit to the number of breaths a man breathes
We do not have to ask learned men about truths like these.
Brother, Maya hath spread its deception everywhere;
Those it blinds forget His Name.
For them there is no peace in this life
And in life hereafter it will be the same.

Once born, man has to live to the end of his days,
To sustain himself for that span of time.
Man goes alone to the place of reckoning when he dies
The wailings of those he leaves behind are but
    meaningless cries.

Everyone says the Lord is great,
None will be outdone in praising Him;
Yet no one has discovered His real worth.
His stature increased by praise.
The worlds are packed with a multitude of people
But Thou alone art our Lord and Master,
Thou alone art the Truth.

Of the low castes mine is the lowest,
I am the meanest of the mean.
O Nanak, amongst the poor seek thy friends and
    companions

Emulate not the mighty.
Where the fallen have protected been
There is Thy grace and mercy seen.

* * *

Jal moh ghas mas kar mat kagad kar sar

Burn away attachment to things of the world
Crush its soot to make ink;
Use your understanding as if it were a sheet of paper,
With the pen of love
Your mind the scribe
And the guru to guide you
Write down your thoughts.

Write the Name of the Lord
Write praises of the Lord
Write that He is without end and without limit.

Brother, if you learn to write all these things
Yours will be the password at the place of reckoning.

You will be acclaimed with honour.
A joyous welcome you will receive,
On your forehead will be the mark of approval
If in the Name of the True One you truly believe.

This is the gift of grace
Idle prattle is all else.

One comes, another goes;
Some style themselves as sardars
Others are destined to beg
Yet others hold grand *darbars*.
Man will know this truth when he dies
That without the Name nothing avails
(Without the Name all else is lies).

Thy might strikes terror in my heart,
My body wastes away in fear of Thee.
Proud, titled Khans and Sultans have I seen
Reduced to dust.

O Nanak, many have I seen pack up and go
I have seen the bonds of false love cut asunder.

* * *

Avauh bhainey gal milauh ank saheladeeah

Come my sister
Let us embrace!
Come beloved friend
Let us speak of love!
Let us sit together
And talk of our Husband
Our perfect, powerful Lord.
Lord, Thou art the Truth,
Thou, the repository of goodness,
We the repositories of evil,
Thou art the Creator
And all is within Thy power.
By Thy One Name we abide
When Thou art there
Why need we think of anyone beside?
Go ask the happy spouse,
'What virtues earned you favour of the Lord?'
(She will tell thee)
'It's the gentle path of *sahaj*, calmness of manner and
    sweetness of tongue.'
If you hearken unto the guru's word

You will meet your Husband, the Lord of Love.

Manifold is Thy nature, Great is Thy bounty
Manifold Thy creatures who praise Thee day and night.
Manifold Thy shapes and colours
Manifold Thy races and castes.

On meeting the true guru
One gains knowledge of the truth
Then one merges into the Truthful One.
From the guru's teaching we learn the fear of the Lord.
From comprehension of the truth we gain honour.

O Nanak! Truth is the king of kings
He taketh us and uniteth us with Him.

* * *

Dhat milai phun dhat kau sifti sifat samai

As pieces of metal of the same kind melt into one
    another,
So a worshipper merges his personality in the object
    of his worship.
Like the dark red of the poppy flower
Is he dyed in the fast colours of truth.
He who in repose and single-minded meditation
Prays to the Truthful One
Becomes one with the Lord.

O brother! Be as the dust under the feet of saints.
In the company of the saintly you'll find
Your guru and the gift of salvation,
You will get *Kamadhenu*, the celestial cow,
The giver of all things desired.
High in the heavens
In setting paradisal
Stands the mansion of the Lord.
A truthful life and good deeds done
Earn us the right to human birth;
By love we find our way
To the gate of the Lord's mansion.
The saintly train their minds to ponder
On the all-pervading soul in meditation.

If we live by the threefold fruits of Karma
(the good, the neutral and the bad)
We shall be victims of hopes and anxieties.
How can one escape the stranglehold of this triple noose?
How find the gentle path of *sahaj* and peace
Save by guidance of the guru?

(Under the guidance of the guru)
We know that in our own home
Stands the mansion of the Lord.
We can invoke His grace
And be cleansed of our sins.

Without the guru's help we cannot wash off the dirt of
    the world,
Without the Lord's grace how can we our haven find?
Abandon hope in other things
On the Divine Word fix your mind.

Sacrificed to that guru may Nanak's life be
Who having himself seen the Lord
Shows others how to see.

* * *

Tan jal bal nati bhaia, man maya moh manoor

My body is burnt to ashes and mingled with dust
My mind is rusted with attachment to worldly things;
Once again my sins pursue me
And falsehood trumpets its victory.
Without the Word we are caught in the wheel
(Of birth, death and rebirth).
Thus hath double-minded duality
Been the undoing of multitudes.
My soul, fix thy mind on the Word Divine
The Word will take thee across the waters of life.
Those who the guru's teaching do not know
Will die and be reborn, go and come, come and go.
A person is pure
If he enshrines the True Name within him.

His body is imbued with the fear of the True One
And his tongue loves the taste of truth.
He, by God's grace, is in a state of ecstasy
His body is of passions free.
The True One made the air,
From air came water
From the waters He made the three regions
In every heart He lit His lamp.
The Lord is Pure, He cannot be defiled.
He who is dyed in the colours of the Lord
Will be honoured (and remain unsullied).

The mind is the true abode of peace
Therein comes the grace of the Lord
The five elements of his body
Are tempered in the fear of the True One
The light of Truth illumines his mind.
O Nanak! his sins are forgiven
And the guru preserves his honour.

* * *

Nanak bedi sach ki bhareeai gur veechar

Sayeth Nanak: Launch the boat of truth with thoughts
    of the guru.
One comes into the world, another goes
Everyone full of self-esteem.

A closed and stubborn mind will sink thy vessel,
But truth of the guru's teaching will take it across.

Without the guru to guide me
How can I cross over to the other shore?
How can I reach the haven of peace?
Lord, preserve me if so Thy pleasure be
I have no other Protector save Thee.

Facing me I see a forest on fire
Behind me I see new life in green.
(And I know thereby that) life begins as it ends
(From God it's born, into God it blends).
Let Truth in every heart be instilled.

He is the Uniter, He makes the union
He takes us to His mansion.
Let every breath I take breathe Thy Name
Lord, let me never forget Thee.

The more my Master possesses my mind
The more I imbibe the nectar of my guru's message.

Lord, to Thee I surrender my body and my mind
Thou art my Master.

Lord, destroy Thou my self-esteem
And let me mingled be in Thee.

He who created this world
Created also the three regions.
Men of God see the Divine Light
They that turn their backs on God
Stumble in darkness.

In every heart shines the Light Eternal
Through the guru's guidance can it be discerned.

Praise be to the saintly who know God
They are blended with the True One
Their true worth shines forth.

O Nanak! His Name doth such peace bring
For the body and soul are in His keeping.

* * *

Ik til pyara veesrai rog vadda man mah

If I forget the Beloved even for a trice
A serious sickness afflicts my soul.
If Hari dwell not within my mind
In His court no place of honour will I find.

On meeting the guru we find peace
Hunger's fire is doused by the waters of virtue.
O heart! Day and night sing praises of God.
Rare in the world are people
Who forget not the Name for even a moment.

Blend your light with the Light Eternal
Mingle your consciousness with His—and see
Violence, selfhood, wanderings of the mind
Anxiety and sorrow will cease to be.
By the grace of the guru meet the saintly
In whose hearts dwells Hari the Lord.

If I offer my body as if it were a bride
The Lord will take it as if He were the groom.
Love not a mortal who you know
Is here for a while as in a passing show.
The saintly blend with the Lord
The virtuous share His couch and become one with Him.

With the sacred water given by the guru
Quench the four fires (of cruelty and anger, of greed
    and love of worldly things).
The lotus which is within thee will blossom
And thy heart will fill with ambrosia.
O Nanak! Make the true guru thy friend
He will take thee to the court of the True One.

* * *

Hari Hari japaoh pyariah gurmat ley Hari bol

Beloved friend, on thy lips ever be the Name of God!
Heed the advice of the guru and call on Hari!
Test thy mind with the touchstone of truth

See that it is of perfect weight,
The mind is a priceless gem
No one has valued it.

O Brother! The gem that is Hari
Is in possession of the guru.
By associating with men of God thou wilt find the
    true guru.
And day and night thou wilt sing songs of praise.

In the light of the guru's teaching
Truthful be thy trade
Truthful too thy earnings.

As fire is put out by water
So will desire be subdued
And become the slave of thy slave.
The demon of death will not pursue thee
Thou wilt swim across the fearful ocean of life.

Men of God like not falsehood
Being themselves true, they love the truthful.
Those who worship mammon, love not the truth
Falsehood's mansion is raised on a false foundation.

Those imbued with truth, meet the guru
The truthful blend with the Truthful One.

In our minds is embedded the gem, the ruby of the Name,

It is a nugget, a diamond beyond all price.
Truth be our investment and our merchandise
The Name of the Lord the treasure we earn.
In the depth of every heart dwells the Lord
O Nanak! The saintly guru and guide we find
If the priceless gem that is Hari be kind.

* * *

Bharmai bhah na vijhvai je bhave disantar des

The fire of pride is not extinguished
By wandering over distant lands.
The dirt of the mind is not cleansed
By wearing clean garments.
Fie, the life of falsehood! Fie, the mask of divinity!

Nothing will make thee a *Bhakta* true
Save the teaching of the true guru.
O mind! If thou seekest good and annihilate pride
Let the guru's word find a place in thine heart
And the craving of the ego will be destroyed.

The mind is a priceless pearl
With it thou canst acquire an honoured place beside
    the Master.
In the company of the pious seek the Lord
For the Lord loves those on whose lips is His Name.
Thy pride shall vanish, and thine be the bliss

Of a wave mingling back into the waters.
Those that have not brought the thought of Hari to
 their minds
Shall be caught in the cycle of birth and death.

Those that come not to the True One, the Supreme Being,
Shall be ruined and like flotsam drift.
On the turbulent waters of life
Human life which is priceless beyond compare
Will thus be bartered away for a worthless shell.

Those to whom the true guru tells the secret,
Acquire complete wisdom.
The guru takes them across the waters
And they are received with honour.
O Nanak! Their faces are radiant
And in their hearts is joy,
Born of the music of His Word.

* * *

Dhan joban ar phulda natheedai din char

Wealth, youth and flowers
Are short-lived—as guests for four brief days.
As leaves of a water-hyacinth taken out of water wither
So wither they.
Dear friend! Make merry while the sap of youth
 courses in your veins

Your days shorten and weariness will overtake your
   ageing body.

My friend once so gay
Has gone to sleep in his grave;
A wretched outcaste that I am,
I too will follow him
Wailing in my feeble voice.
My soul! My fair one! Didst thou not hear
With thine own ear
Not forever is the bliss of the parental home?
For thy groom (death) awaits thee there?

O Nanak! In her father's home she slept
So carefree as if the night were endless;
In broad daylight was she robbed
Her dowry of goodness was thus lost
And her sack filled with sin.

* * *

Tu daryao dana bina mai machali kaisey ant lahah

Lord, Thou art the mighty river,
Thou knowest and seest all things.
How can I, a poor fish know
Thy depth and Thy expanse?

Whichever way I turn,

There art Thou and no other.
Taken away from Thine waters,
I suffocate and die.

I know not the fisherman
I see not his net.
But when I am caught in it
In my black agony
It is to Thee I turn.

Lord, Thou who art present everywhere,
In my folly I believed Thou wert far from me.
Whatever I do is known to Thee
When Thou seest all
How can I deny my deeds?

I am not worthy to serve Thee,
I cannot glorify Thy Name.
Whatever Thou givest
That will I eat;
I beg at no other door but Thine.
Nanak hath but one petition
Let his body and soul be in Thine keeping.

He is near, He is far.
He is midway between the two;
All that He has created in the world
He watches and He hears.

O Nanak! What He wills
Comes to pass.

* * *

Achal chalai na chalai

He deprives of delusion
The things that delude;
He blunts the edge of the dagger
And it does not wound.
Man's mind wavers for it is full of craving;
He is safe only in the Lord's keeping.

How then light the lamp when there is no oil?
Let your body be the lamp,
From the holy books take wisdom
And use it as oil.
Let knowledge of His presence be the wick
And with the tinder of truth
Strike the spark.
Thus light you the oil-lamp
And in its light meet your Lord.

When the recording Angel claims your body
And catalogues your deeds,
Your good acts will save you from the cycle of birth
and death.

If in life you have served others
Your reward shall be a place in His court.
Says Nanak: You will raise your arms in joy.

* * *

Akh akh man vavana jeo jeo japai vai

Let your heart sing of God with every breath you draw;
How great is He whom we serenade? Where does
    He live?
All those that sang Thy praise are now in deep meditation.
Brother! Allah is beyond our reach and beyond limit
Pure is His Name; pure His abode, He is in truth our
    Preserver.
How great is Thy dominion cannot be known; no one
    knows how to write of it:
A hundred bards singing in chorus could not describe
    a fraction of Thy greatness.
Nobody hath found Thy worth; everyone repeats what
    he has heard another say.

Saints, prophets, guides (who show the way to God),
Men of faith, men of God and martyrs
Preachers, seekers and law-givers
Guardians of mosques and the Darvesh who are
    welcomed at God's gate,
Gain greater blessing.

Their lives are like the additional prayer when worship
    is over.

He asks no one when He builds; He asks no one when
    He destroys;
He asks no one when He gives or takes.
He knows His own creation; He acts and causes others
    to act.
He extends His grace to everyone; and favours those
    who please Him.
We know not His dwelling; we know not His Name.
We know not how great His Name is among other names.

How great is the place where lives my Lord, the king
    of kings?
None can reach it; of whom shall I ask the way?
When God raises one caste above others,
Those not raised do not like it.
Greatness is in the hands of the Great One; He gifts to
    whom He pleases.

He sees that His rule obtains everywhere; He brooks
    no delay.
Everyone cries for more hoping thereby to increase
    his share.
How great is Thy bounty, Thou giver of countless gifts!

Nanak, from age to age, never does His storehouse
diminish.

* * *

Sabhe kant maheliya saglia karah seegar

We are His wives; we adorn ourselves for Him.
We dress ourselves in bright red to gain His attention
But love is not won by bargaining; a counterfeit coin
gilded with gold is soon found out and spells ruin.
How does a woman win the attention of the Lord?
Lord, she who is pleasing to Thy sight is in nuptial bliss;
Thy mercy is her adornment.

The guru's word is her adornment; her body and soul
are with her Lord.
With hands clasped she waits on Him; her prayer
comes from the truthfulness of her heart.
She is immersed in His love, she lives in fear of the
True One;
And when dyed with His love, her colour is fast and true.
She is counted among the followers of the Beloved.
She is recognized as one of His hand-maidens.
Her love is not sundered; the True One unites her with
Himself.
Her soul is plaited with the Word
I am ever a sacrifice unto her.

She who is absorbed in the true guru becomes immortal,
    never shall she become a widow.
Her Beloved is forever handsome and renews
His youth; He does not die nor depart.
He ever enjoys His fulfilled wife; His gracious eyes
    rest on her ever-obedient person.
Truth is in the plaits of her hair, love in her dress and
    ornaments,
God within her is like the breath of sandal perfume,
    her chamber has the tenth gate
    (through which the Lord enters).

She lights the lamp of the Word, she wears God's name
    as her necklace.
She is beautiful amongst women of beauty; on her
    forehead she wears the jewel of love.
Her beauty and wisdom are bewitching, her love is
    true and infinite.
She knows no man besides her Beloved; it is only for
    the true guru that she has love and affection.

Why did you waste the dark night in sleep?
How will you pass the hours without your Lord?
Woman, your bosom shall be afire, your body burn,
    and your mind be aflame.
A woman not taken by her Husband wastes away her
    youth.

Her Husband is on her couch; but she sleeps and knows
    not of His presence.
I sleep while my Beloved is awake; to whom shall I
    turn for advice?
Sayeth Nanak, the true guru teaches how to fear and
    love God
And thus be united with Him.

* * *

Macchli jal na janian sar khara asgah

A fish in the deep and salty sea
Very wise and pretty was she,
How was it then that she was taken unawares
And knew not of the net?
She suffered for her acts
None can escape the noose of death.
Brothers, know that the angel of death hovers above you.
As on the fish so on us men
When we least expect it
Will fall the net.

The entire world is within death's compass
Without the guru there is no means of combating it.
By truth gain release
Through truth dispel doubt and duality
My life be a sacrifice to the truthful

Who have reached the gate of the True One.
As a small bird in the talons of a hawk,
Or on the ground caught in the huntsman snare
So is man in the thrall of death.
Only those the guru protects are saved.
If ye have not the Name
You will be picked out and destroyed
You will have no friends or companions to help you.

He is True,
His realm is Truth.
Those who have faith in Him
Are pure of heart.
Those who have gained this knowledge from the guru
Are true and speak the truth.

Thus do I pray to the true guru:
'Take me to the Lord and unite me with Him,'
On being united, I will gain peace,
The demon of death will poison himself and die,
'Let me abide by the Name
And let the Name abide in me.'

Without the guru we stumble in the dark,
Without the Word there is no understanding,
The guru's teaching illumines the mind
And attaches it to the truth
Then hath death no dominion

Our light blends with the Light Eternal.

Thou art our Companion, Thou art wise,
Thou art Thyself the Uniter.
Through the teaching of the guru
We exalt Thee who hast no end nor limit.
Where there is the immortal Word of the guru
Death shall have no dominion.

By His ordinances comes all creation into being,
By His ordinances all labour and earn.
Under His ordinance is death,
By His ordinance we mingle with Truth.
O Nanak! Whatever pleases Him comes to pass
We mortals by ourselves can do nothing.

* * *

Jap tap sanjam sadheeai teerath keechai vas

Prayer, austerity, control over the senses
Pilgrimages to holy places,
Giving of alms, charity and all other good deeds,
What matter they unless they gain merit
With the Lord who is Truth?

As you sow, so shall you reap
Life without virtue is life without hope.

Young woman understand
If thou becomest the hand-maiden of good deeds
Thou shalt attain peace and joy.
Abandon evil ways, merge with the Lord
And find fulfilment in the teaching of the guru.

Without goods to sell, a trader sits idly staring in all
  directions
He knows not how to start, his merchandise earns no
  profit.
Without anything to trade in, he suffers heavy losses.
Thus one who trades in falsehood suffers
And is afflicted with sorrow.

If he looks within himself
And examines the gem in his heart
He will earn much profit.
Days and nights will bring increase in his income
He will take home his earnings
And thus depart with his affairs settled.

Tradesman, let thy trade be under the guidance of saints,
Meditate upon the Creator.
If it please God the Uniter
You will meet men of God.
He in whom is lit the light Eternal
Will never thereafter suffer separation.

Truth will be his prayer-mat
Truthful his life,
True his love and adoration.

Those who recognize their real selves
Their hearts become the abode of God.
They take on the hues of the True One
The True One becomes their gain.

In the three regions, He alone is the Supreme Lord,
He is the Truth, His Name is Truth.

A wife who knows the company of her Husband
Who is sent for by Him to His mansion
And with whom He disports Himself
Is in veritable bliss.
Call her happy, call her true
She hath won her Lord's heart by her virtue.

I stumble in the desert wastes
From deserts I clamber up the hills;
I lose myself in the forests.
Without the guru to guide me
I shall not find my way.
If thus I wander everywhere
I shall come and go from life to life.

Go, ask travellers who tread the path of servitude,
How to recognize our Sovereign Lord.

How to gain admission to his mansion
Without being questioned at the gates.
O Nanak! The One Lord reigns supreme everywhere
There is no second person, there is no other.

* * *

Sun man bhooley bavrey gur ki charni lag

Thou simple, stupid soul
Hearken unto me!
Attach thyself to the feet of the guru
Pray to Hari, ponder over His Name.
The demon of death will be affeared of Thee
Sorrows will flee from thee.

A woman with dual loyalties suffers much;
How can she remain happily married?
Brother! I have no other sanctuary
Save His Name; it is my only treasure.
My guru gave it to me
I am forever beholden to him.

Through the guru's teaching we attain honour
To the guru be all praise for uniting me to Him.
Without Him I would not live a single watch of the day,
Without the name I would surely perish.
Blind am I, let me not lose sight of the Name;

Let my mind be steadfast when I leave for my last
   journey.

Those whose gurus are themselves blind
Pointless is their pursuit (of Truth)
Without guidance of the true guru
We cannot find the Name.
Without the Name life hath no purpose.
It's birth and death and regret
It is like the cawing of a crow in a deserted house.

Without the Name the body is like a hall of sorrows
With its walls eaten up by dry rot;
We cannot reach His abode
Unless there is truth in our hearts.
If we are imbued with the Name
In our own homes we attain salvation.

I enquired of my guru,
By his direction I earned my life's wages.
Ego that fouled my soul,
Ego that caused sorrow
Was thus burnt out by the Word of God.
By the gentle path of *sahaj* did I meet Him,
Purified by truth I merged in the Truest of the True.

Those imbued with the Word are without stain,
They lust no more,

They conquer anger and pride;
They worship Thy name a hundred times and more
And have Hari enshrined in their hearts.
Why forget Him who sustains life?

He who dies with the divine Word on his lips
Dies to death
He need not die a second time.
Only through the Word shall we find Him
And learn the love of prayer.
Without the Word, people wander in error
They die only to be reborn, over and over again.
Everyone praises himself
From being great he becomes greatest of the great.
Without the guru's help he knows not his real self,
He only hears what others say about him.
O Nanak! He who knows the Word
Never thereafter talks of himself.

* * *

Satgur poora je milai paeeiai ratan beechar

If we find the true, the perfect guru
Our thoughts become priceless as a ruby;
If we present our minds to the guru
We are rewarded with all-embracing love,
We get the gift of salvation

The Forgiver forgives us our sins.

O brother! Know that without the guru there is no
    knowledge
Go ask Brahma, Narad and Vyasa, ask anyone.
The guru gives us knowledge and power to concentrate,
The guru makes the incomprehensible capable of
    understanding.
The guru is like the tree in full leaf casting a vast shade,
The guru's treasury is full of rubies, gems and other
    precious stones.
In the guru's treasury is the Name unsullied and pure
    love
(From it we can borrow)
Trade in truth
And earn profit beyond reckoning.
The true guru is the giver of joy
And the dispeller of sorrows.

He is the destroyer of the five demons of sin
    (lust, anger, greed, attachment and pride).
The ocean of life is terrifying and difficult to cross.
We can see neither the land behind us nor the opposite
    shore,
Neither boat nor raft, neither an oar nor a boatman.
Let the fear of the true guru be our boat.
By His grace He will take us across.

If for a trice you forget the Beloved Lord
Sorrow will afflict you, joy will depart.
Burn the wretched tongue which loves not repeating
the Name.
The body's earthen vessel cracks, it is wracked with pain,
The demon of death grabs you, your regrets are then
in vain.

All our lives we cry; 'this is mine' and depart crying,
'this too is mine'.
We discover that neither body, nor wealth, nor wife
was ours to take away.
There is no wealth except the Name;
(Without the Name) we are lost in the maze of maya
Serve the Master who is Truth
The guru will tell you of One who is beyond telling.

On the wheel of birth, death and rebirth
Are our natures moulded
And the pattern of our lives determined.
What is writ cannot be erased by anyone,
For it is the dictate of the Lord.

Without the Name of Hari there is no escape
(From the cycle of birth, death and rebirth)
The teaching of the guru shows the way to union divine.

I have no one save the Lord

My life and soul belong to Him.
I have burnt away my ego
I have burnt my greed and pride.
Sayeth Nanak, ponder over the Name Divine
The treasure of virtues will all be thine.

* * *

Re man Hari seo aisee preet kar jaisee jal kamleh

My soul hearken unto me!
Love thy Lord as the lotus loves water
Buffeted by waves its affection does not falter.
Creatures that have their being in water,
Taken out of water, die.
My soul! If thou hast not such love
How wilt thou obtain release?
If the Word of the guru is within us
We shall accumulate a store of devotion.

My soul hearken unto me!
Love thy Lord as a fish loves water.
The more the water, the greater its joy,
Greater the tranquillity of its body and mind.
Without water it cannot live one watch of the day
Only God knows the anguish of its heart.

My soul hearken unto me!
Love thy Lord as the *Chatrik* loves the rain.

Although the lakes be full, the plains flooded and green
It will not drink one drop.
By God's grace, its thirst will be slaked
But destiny may doom it to die.

My soul hearken unto me!
Love thy Lord as water loves milk.
It takes on the heat, boils and evaporates before the
    milk can suffer.
He alone unites, He alone separates
He alone bestows true greatness.

My soul hearken unto me!
Love thy Lord as the *Chakvi* loves the sun
It sleeps not a wink for the distant sun it deems close.
The perverse of mind know not that the godly are ever
    in His presence.
The perverse of mind make many calculations
What the Creator does comes to pass.
Much as all desire to evaluate Him, He cannot be
    evaluated.
Through the teaching of the guru can He be found
And with the True One comes tranquillity.

If the true guru presents it, true love will not sunder
We are given the gift of knowledge and learn the secret
    of the three worlds.

If we trade in goodness, we shall not forget the Name
that is pure.

Birds that fed on land and water have sported and left
their feeding ground.
We are here a watch or two on borrowed time; our
sport is also for the day and the morrow.
He whom Thou unitest with Thyself find their true
abode.

Without the guru, love cannot be born
The dross of the ego cannot be rinsed away.
He who recognizes the God within
Understands the secret of the Word and is happy.

Disciples of the guru know their real selves,
No need have they for anyone's help.

Why speak of those who are already one with God?
They have the Word and are fulfilled.
The perverse of mind do not comprehend,
They are separated from God and suffer.
O Nanak! There is but one gate to the Lord's mansion
And there is no other sanctuary.

* * *

Ram nam man bedhiya, avar ki kari vichar

My heart is pierced by the Name of Rama! What else
    shall I reflect upon?
Tranquil is the mind which meditates on the Word,
Happy is the one who is imbued with God.
Preserve me as it pleases Thee,
Thy Name, O Hari, is my support.
My soul, the will of the Master is just.
Attach thyself to Him who made thy body and mind
    and adorned it.

Were I to weigh my body, cut into tiny pieces and
    burn in a sacrificial fire;
Were I to turn my body and soul into firewood, burn it
    every day;
Were I to light hundreds of thousands of sacrificial
    fires, they would not equal the Name of Hari.

Were my head sawed in twain, my torso torn in two;
Were my body frozen in Himalayan snows,
It would not rid my mind of disease.
No remedy equals the Name of Hari
This have I tested and found true.

Were I to give away castles of gold,
Strings of horses of good pedigree
And mighty elephants;

Were I to make gifts of land and of herds of cows.
I would be aware of my goodness
And pride would remain in my heart.
The guru has given me the true gift;
My mind is pierced by the Name of Rama.

How many hard-headed thinkers are there?
How many interpretations of the Vedas?
In how many fetters is the soul bound?
The gate of salvation is only reached through the guru's
    instruction.
Truth is above all; above truth is truthful conduct.

Call everyone exalted; let no one appear to thee low.
The One God fashioned the vessels,
One source of light illumines the three worlds,
By His grace we find the truth; what He gives once
    none can take away.

When a good man meets a saint
He gains the guru's affection
And attains tranquillity.
If we are absorbed in the true guru, we can meditate in
    matters beyond the realm of speech.
He who drinks the nectar of the Name shall find
    fulfilment,
He shall go to God's court wearing robes of honour.

In the hearts of those who love the Word, reverberate
  strains of the lute.
Few there are who hearken to the guru's words
  everyday and obtain understanding.
O Nanak! Forget not the Name, let the Word be thy
  wage and gain release.

* * *

Chite disai dhaulhar bage bank duar

Behold, gilded mansions with white ornamented gates!
Knowing they are perishable and delude us into love
  of worldly things
Our eyes rejoice at the sight.
Likewise the human body; it shall decay and be
  mingled with the dust.
If it hath love in it, nothing else will remain.
Listen brother! Neither thy body nor thy wealth will
  accompany thee.
The Name of Rama is real wealth; God gives it through
  the guru.
If the Giver gives real wealth of the Name of Rama
He who is befriended by the guru and the Creator shall
  not be questioned in the world to come.

If God wills it, we shall be liberated; God alone can
  pardon us.

The fool believes that daughters, sons and relations
    belong to him;
He sees his wife and is pleased. He knows not that she
    who brings joy, also brings sorrow.
Men of God are imbued with the Word, day and night
    imbibe Hari's ambrosia.

The mind of the unbeliever wavers and wanders in the
    futile quest after wealth.
We waste ourselves in looking all round while the Real
    Thing is within us.
The perverse preoccupied with themselves do not see it;
The saintly secure it in their aprons.

Infidel, who art without virtue, learn thy true origin!
The body which is compounded of blood and semen
    shall be burnt in fire.

Thy body is at the mercy of breath
It will last as long as it is fated to last.
We pray for long life; no one seeks death.
Only he can be described as happy who through the
    guru's teaching has God in his heart.
Worthless is life without the Name,
Wasted is life if it gains not a vision of God.
As a man knows not his state when he sleeps at night,
So one who hath pride in his heart knows not that he is
    in the coils of duality and maya's serpent.

Hearken to the teaching of your guru,
Ponder on the nature of this world
And you will see that life and the world are as dreams.

As the fire of thirst is slaked by water,
As mother's milk is to her hungry child,
As the lake is to the lotus and the fish,
Without which they die—
So is the nectar or Hari's Name given by the guru,
    sayeth Nanak.
'May my life be spent singing the songs of the Lord.'

* * *

Doongar dekh daravano paeidai daryas

The mountain of life is awesome; I watch it from my
    father's house and am terrified.
It is steep and difficult to ascend; there is no ladder to
    climb.
I took my guru's teaching to my heart; the guru united
    me to God and I was saved.
Brother! The ocean of life is fearful and hard to cross!
If the perfect, the true guru, in his pleasure receives me,
He will take me across on the Name of God.
If all I do is to say 'I have to go'
It will be of no avail.
If in fact I realize that death is certain

(Then I really know).
Everyone who comes into the world must go;
Only God and the guru are immortal.
Praise the True One,
Cherish the place where His praise is sung.

Beautiful gateways,
Houses and palaces
Strongholds by the thousand;
Elephants and horses richly caparisoned,
Hundreds of thousands of troops—beyond all count.
Not one of these will accompany you on your last journey.
The fool pines away for them and dies in his ignorance.

Man amasses gold and silver,
He knows not that wealth is an entangling net.
Man may have his dominion proclaimed by beat of
    drum throughout the whole world.
He knows not that without the Name death will ever
    hover about his head.
When the body collapses, the game of life is over,
What then shall be the state of the evil-doers?

Man delights when he sees his sons
Has the sight of his wife on her couch;
He wears perfumes of aloe and sandal; he dresses in
    fine clothes and ornaments

Yet shall he leave his home and family; dust must
    return to dust.

However great the title—chief, emperor or raja.
Governor, khan, headman or chieftain,
These are but faggots in the fire of pride.
Turn your face against God and ye shall be
As stalks of pampas in a forest fire.

Whoever comes into the world
Shall depart;
However proud he be,
Must die and go.
The whole world is as a chamber black with soot;
The body and soul which enter it are also blackened.
Only they whom the guru preserves remain clean
For the fire of desires is extinguished by prayer.

O Nanak! We cross the ocean of life by the True Name
    of God who is the king of kings!
May I not forget the Name of Hari; may the Name of
    Hari be as a jewel of my purchase.
The perverse perish in the terrible ocean of the world;
Only men of God cross the fathomless sea.

* * *

Paunai pani agni ka mel

Air, water and fire
Of these elements is our body made
Within it is the restless agitation of the mind.
It has nine doorways
The tenth is the one through which one goes to meet God.
O learned one, have you thought of this?

Everyone can discourse, speak and listen.
Only he who thinks for himself is a true scholar
And a learned divine.

The body is made of clay
The sounds that emerge are of substance airy.
Know you, O learned one,
What dies when a man does *die*?

Consciousness dies
Then dies the ego
But the soul, it dies not.

What seek you in pilgrimage to sacred rivers?
The priceless jewel is enthroned within your breast.
The learned pandit reads much, declaims much
But knows not of the treasure within.

It is not I who die.
But the demon of ignorance who is destroyed;

The soul that sustains me dies not.

Says Nanak, this is what the Lord the Creator has
  shown me

Now I know there is neither birth nor death.

* * *

Jato jae kahan te avai

Know you whence comes life?

How we are born? Where we go when we die?

Why some are caught in the cycle of birth and rebirth

While others are freed to merge in the Deathless One?

Those who have Him in their hearts

And have His Name ever on their lips;

Those who worship Him but seek no return

To them gently comes birth and death.

Thoughts arise in the mind, in the mind do they subside.

Only the guru's word gives us freedom,

Contemplating upon it, we achieve deliverance.

Like birds at dusk settling on trees

To roost for the night

Some joyous, some sorrowing; all lost in themselves.

When dawns the day and gone is the night

They look up at the sky and resume their wayward flight.

So does man fulfil his destiny.

Those who through the Lord's Name have knowledge
Know that the world is but a temporary shepherd's hut
In a pastureland.

Man is a vessel overflowing with lust and anger.
Without stores the shop looks desolate
And so does the home
So also the human frame without the treasure trove of
    the Name.
The guru breaks down the massive walls of ignorance.

By virtue of your past deeds you meet the holy,
Truly joyful are godly men.
Those that gently give up their bodies and soul to the Lord
At their feet will Nanak prostrate himself.

* * *

Amrit kaya rahai sukhali baji eh sansaro

Lookest thou upon thyself as immortal?
Art thou happy in that fond delusion?
The entire world plays this game of make-believe
Thus hunger, greed and untruth we earn in ample measure.

O body of mine! I have seen thee humbled,
I have seen thee as dust upon the face of the earth.
My soul, hearken to these words of mine!
Good deeds will abide with thee

But thou wilt not again have the opportunity to perform
    them.

I speak to thee, my body
Hearken unto these words of mine!
Do not speak evil of others, pry not into their affairs
Create not mischief and destroy confidence among
    people.
Go not unto other men's wives,
Steal not nor commit other evil deeds
Thy soul like the swan will fly away,
Leaving thee widowed and untenanted in the world.

O body of mine! Thou livest in a dream-world,
What merit didst thou earn for thyself?
It replied: 'I stole whatever pleased my fancy
I earned no merit in this life,
I gained no moorings in the life to come,
Thus did I waste away my human birth.
O Baba Nanak, I was really caught in two minds
And no one heeded my plight.'

'Strings of horses I had, of Tadjik and Turkish blood
Gold and silver I had, I was rich in raiment.
O Nanak, none of these could I take with me.
All had to be shed, all went to waste.
Crystallized sugar and dried fruits, I tasted all
They did not last,

I found that only the Name of the Lord is immortal.'

'Deep foundations I dug
And on them raised high walls;
But the temple I built collapsed in a rubbled heap.
I hoarded my treasure, I gave nothing away.
I was blind, I believed it was mine to keep
Then like the golden Lanka all was gone.'

O foolish, ignorant soul listen to me!
Only the Lord's will comes to pass.
Our Master is a great Merchant Prince,
We His travelling salesmen,
Our souls and bodies are His investment
He fills and re-animates as He wills.

* * *

Avar panch ham ek jana keo rakhao ghar bar mana

They were five, I was alone
How could I guard my home and my possessions?
They beat and looted me again and again,
To whom shall I lodge a complaint?

My soul! Repeat the Name of Rama
Facing thee is the army of Yama,
The god of death.

He raised the body like a house with many gates
Within He put the soul as housewife.
While she disports herself believing the house and all
    it has
Is hers forever
The five are forever plundering her.

Death demolished the house,
Looted all therein,
And took the housewife captive.
Death beat her with a rod
And put a chain around her neck.
The five took to their heels and fled.
A wife wants silver and gold,
Friends ask for food and drink,
O Nanak, one who sins for such cheap gains
Shall go to his doom bound in chains.

                        * * *

Rain gavaee soi ke divas gavaya khae

I wasted my nights in sleep
The days I wasted eating and enjoying,
The priceless gift of life
I bartered away for a cowrie shell.

I knew not the Name of Rama
Fool! You will regret this hereafter.

Man buries his hoard under the earth.
He seeks not God who is truly without limit.
Those who go into the world seeking gain
Lose the Lord when they return.

If all one desired one got
All of us would be wealthy;
Not by words but by deeds do we reach
The goal for which we aspire.

O Nanak, the Creator takes care
Of what He did create.
We do not comprehend His Ordinances
Nor why He makes some men great.

* * *

Choa chandan ank chadavau, pat patambar
  pehor hadavau

I may perfume my body with scented aloe and sandal
Drape it in silks and satins,
Without the Name of Hari, how shall I find happiness?

What shall I wear? What display?
Without the Lord of the world, how shall I find happiness?

I may wear ring in my ears and a necklace of pearls
  about my neck,

I may sit on a red mattress adorned with poppy flowers,
Without the Lord of the world, how shall I find happiness?

I may possess a beautiful woman with bewitching eyes
Lovelier for the sixteen kinds of beauty aids.
Without the Lord of the world, forever shall I wander
    in frustration.
I may have houses and mansions with luxurious couches
    to recline on,
Gardens with gardeners tending flowerbeds at all hours,
Without the Name of Hari, they will be abodes of sorrow.

I may have horses and elephants, lancers and bondsmen
Militia, mace-bearers and retainers,
Without the Lord of the world, these will be but sham
    display.

I may gain renown as a miracle maker,
Have power to make gold, power to vanish at will.
I may wear a crown on my head and over it a royal
    umbrella to shade me,
Without the Lord of the world, how shall I find truth?

I may be a khan, a chieftain, a king
Order everyone about: 'Come here you! And you!'
It will all be sham display,
Without the guru's word my affairs will not prosper.

By the guru's teaching
I have overcome my ego and my pride;
By the guru's teaching
I know that God the destroyer of demons
Doth within me reside.
Nanak makes this supplications,
'Master I crave Thy protection.'

* * *

Seva ek na janas avrey, parpanch biadh tyagai kavrey

He who serves the One God will know no other,
He does not concern himself with the world's bitterness
 and strife;
By love and truth he is united with the truest of
 the True.
Such a man is a devotee of God,
He sings praises of the Lord;
He washes away the dirt on his person
And makes his Union with God.

The lotus in our hearts is upside down;
The world heeds false messages and burns in error;
Only he who meditates on the guru's words will
 be saved.

The bumble-bee and the moth, the elephant and the fish

Like deer meet their doom because of their own doings.
So it is with men: cravings makes them blind to reality.

Lust fills their hearts; they become lovers of women,
Frustration and anger prove their undoing.
They lose their minds and their poise
Because they forget the Name.

Concern with other people's affairs makes their minds
   wander in error;
They put halters around their necks and are enmeshed
   in troubles.
Only the saintly who sing praises of God escape.

As a widow will for the love of money give her body
   to strangers
So we pledge our minds to others.
Without the Lord as our lover we shall never find
   fulfilment.

Study all the scriptures, all litanies recite
Read all the religious epics and have them explained;
Unless you are dyed in the essence of Truth
Your mind will wobble in error.

As the *Chatrik* bird loves the rain
And cries for a few drops to slake its thirst;
As the fish gambols in the waters,

Nanak is athirst for the Name of Hari,
He drinks and his heart is filled with joy.

* * *

Mundh rain duheladia jeeo need na avai

Long and sleepless is the night (of life)
For a woman separated from the Lord
She wears away pining for Him,
She becomes weak waiting and watching for the return
    of her Spouse.

Her adornments, the sweet delicacies offered to her
Are without taste; life has no purpose for her.
Her youth bursting like heady wine turns sour
But youth returns not; her bosom will not fill again.

Sayeth Nanak: as with a woman so with us all
We shall meet the Lord when He wills,
Else our nights will be long and without sleep.

If the wretched woman be deprived of her Lord and
    Husband
How shall she find fulfilment?
Without her Husband her house will not be a home.
Ask her friends and companions, they will tell you
Without the love of the Name
There is no truth, no life of comfort.

In your heart let there be truth,
Let contentment be your companion,
In your mind the guru's message.
These facilitate union with the Lover, our Husband.
Sayeth Nanak, a woman who never forsakes the Name
Is gently united with her Lord.

Come my friends and companions!
Let us praise the Lord, our Husband.
I will ask my guru and write a message of love to be
    sent to Him,
My guru hath shown me my True Lord.

The perverse of mind will have cause to regret,
My wayward mind has ceased to wander;
It is stilled and I recognize the truth.
The wine of truth renews its strength,
The Word renews the vigour of love;
O Nanak, when the Lord is gracious
Truth is easily comprehended.

'Friends and companions! I am united with the Lord,
My desires are fulfilled,
My Beloved hath come to my home.
Women! Sing hosannas to the Lord
Sing songs of joy and bliss.
The Lord hath fulfilled me.
My sorrows are over.

My friends rejoice
My foes are filled with envy.'
Such a woman's prayer is true
And true her earnings.
With the palms of her hands joined she prays:
'Lord, night and day let me live in Thy love.'
Sayeth Nanak, when man and wife are thus united
Are their desires truly fulfilled.

* * *

Sun nah prabhu jeo ekaldi ban mahe

All alone am I in the wilderness
O Lord, my Husband, listen to me!
How can a wife be free to care
Unless she finds You who are free of all care?

She cannot live without her Husband
Her nights are long and hard to endure
For sleep comes not to her,
O Lord of Love, listen to my prayer!

Only my Love cares for me, none else gives a thought
    to me,
Alone am I in my lamentation.
O Nanak, the fortunate woman has her tryst with her
    Lord
And becomes one with Him.

Without Him her life is indeed a tale of sorrow.

* * *

Sun vadda akhai sab koi

Having heard of Thy greatness
All say Thou art great;
How great Thou art
We shall know when we see Thee;
Thy worth cannot be valued
Thy praise not put into words;
Those who tried to speak of Thee were merged in Thee.

O Great Master of mine! Of wisdom profound, of
   virtues a treasure!
Of Thy great apron none hath the measure.

All learned men with their loads of Vedic learning,
All evaluations put together;
Scholars, thinkers, teachers and those who teachers
   teach
Could not even a sesame seed of Thy greatness gauge.

All charities and giving of alms;
All penances, all that good deeds gain
Praises by Siddhas who perform miracles
   (all, all are in vain)
Without Thy aid Siddhas could no miracles make

None can come between us if Thou art compassionate.
Sorry is the plight of one who tries to contain in words,
Thy treasure is replete with words of praise.
Whom Thou givest the power need try no other ways
'This truth have I beheld,' Nanak says.

* * *

Akhan jivan visrai mar jaun

By prayer I live; without it I die.
The Name of the True One is hard to say
Hunger for the Name of the True One
Fulfils that hunger and sorrows fly away.

Why then forget Him, O mother of mine?
The Lord is true, His Name is Truth divine.

Praise of the True Name is a bare mustard seed
   (of His real greatness)
We'll speak of Him till we are weary of speech,
(We run out of words) and yet not His values reach.
If all together we exalted His nature
It would neither increase nor decrease His stature.

He does not die; He suffers no sorrow
He goes on giving, His bounty never fails,
This virtue alone hath He
None like Him there was before

None like Him shall hereafter be.

Thy bounty is as great as Thy might
Thou madest the day and also the night.
He who forgets Thee is of low birth
O Nanak! one without Name is lowest of the low-born.

* * *

Jeta sabad surat dhun teti jeta rup kaya teri

All the sounds we hear are but a part of the mighty
     roar of Thy torrent,
All the sights we see are but a part of Thy vast creation,
Thou art the taste (in all we taste)
Thou art the fragrance (in all that is fragrant)
O mother of mine! no other hath these qualities.
My Master is One
He is One, brother, the only One.

He is the Destroyer and the Redeemer
He gives and He takes
He regards and rejoices,
He is the granter of grace.

He is the Doer of whatever is to be done,
No one else can make that claim.
As He deals with us, so we speak of Him.
Everything doth His greatness proclaim.

In this dark age man's mind is like a brewer's vat
Filled with the sweet wine of delusion.
Sayeth humble Nanak,
This is also one of Thy many manifestations.

* * *

Niv pae lagau gur apney atam Ram nihariya

I bow low to clasp the feet of my guru,
I have vision of God Rama.
My mind meditated on Him
In my heart I saw and enshrined Him.

Utter the Name of Rama and be saved!
By the guru's grace
The gem that is God you will find,
The darkness of ignorance will be dispelled
And your mind will be illumined.

Mere lip-worship cannot break our fetters
Nor dissipate delusions of the ego;
When we meet the true guru, thoughts of self
     disappear
And we reach our goal.

Those who worship the Name of Hari
Regard Him as their well-beloved Lord;
Their hearts fill with peace

As the oceans fill with water.

The Bountiful Giver of life to the world
Loves those who worship Him.
Let the guru's teaching guide your thinking,
Hari will Himself take you across the ocean of life.

He who kills himself battling his own heart finds God,
In his own mind he vanquishes his cravings.
Sayeth Nanak, if the Lord, Life-of-the-World be kind
The gentle path of prayer we shall find.

* * *

Dudh bin dhen, pankh bin pankhi

A cow that yields no milk
A bird clipped of its wings
Are of as little use as unwatered, withered vegetation;
So like a king to whom no one makes salutation
Is the heart without the Name:
A cell in pitch-black darkness.

When I forget Thee many sorrows assail me
Lord, forsake me not in my afflictions.

My eyes have lost their light
My tongue hath lost its taste
No sounds echo in my ear

With the aid of crutches my feet move forward.
Such is the harvest of bitter fruit reaped by those who
    serve not God.

In the orchard of your heart, O man
Sow seeds of the divine Word!
Water it in plenty with love.
Your trees will bear fruit of the One Name.
If you make not this effort
How do you expect to reap any harvest?

All creatures are Thine
If they serve Thee not,
They will reap no fruit.
Sorrow and joy are as Thou willest
Without Thy Name there is no life.

To kill thoughts of self within oneself
Is true living; there is no other way to live.
Sayeth Nanak, Thou art the Restorer of life
Preserve us as it pleases Thee.

* * *

Kaia Brahma man hai dhoti, gyan janeu dhyan kuspati

If thy body were a Brahmin priest performing ritual
Let thy heart be the dhoti he wears;
Let divine knowledge be thy sacred thread

Meditation the leaf-ring he wears on his finger,
Instead of alms, beg for the name of God and thank
Him.
By the guru's favour you will blend in your Maker.

O pandit priest! Let the Name of God be thy purification,
Let the Name be thy learning, wisdom and way of life.

The sacred thread on the body means little
Unless there be divine light within thee.
Make remembrance of the Name
The mark on thy forehead and thy dhoti.
The Name shall abide by thee in this life
And the life hereafter.
Seek the Name and nothing else besides.
With love in thy heart worship the Lord
And burn away love for wealth.
Seek only the One, seek no other.
See the essence of reality
Through the vault that opens the tenth gate
Repeat His Name and upon it meditate.
If love be thy sacred food
Fear and superstition will flee;
If the watchman is wakeful
Thieves will not break in at night.
Let knowledge that God is One be the mark
on your forehead

Consciousness of the God within the essence of learning.

No one can win favour with God by mere performance
of ritual;

Mere recitation of sacred texts does not reveal His worth

His secrets are not unravelled by the eighteen Puranas
or the four Vedas.

Sayeth Nanak, only the true guru can show you the
Creator.

* * *

Kachi gagar deh duheli upjal binsai dukh pae

The body is like a pitcher of soft clay filled with sorrow;
It is made and unmade
And each time it suffers.
This world is like a turbulent sea,
How shall we swim in it?
Without the help of God and the guru
We will not find the opposite shore.

Except Thee I have no other, my Beloved!
O Hari, except Thee I have no other!
Thou giveth colour to all that is colourful
Thou giveth shape to everything that hath shape;
Thou forgiveth those on whom descends Thy grace.

Maya is like a wicked mother-in-law
Who will not let me make a home

Nor let me meet my Lord and Husband.
(In gratitude) shall I clasp the feet of my friends and
    companions.
For by the kindness of my guru
The Lord hath looked upon me with favour
And I shall be saved.

I meditated
I conquered my mind and perceived
There is no greater friend than Thou.
As you ordain, so shall I live.
Sorrow and joy you apportion, I'll accept.
Hopes and ambitions have I dispelled
I'll seek neither the good nor the neutral nor the evil
The blessed fourth stage I'll find in the guru's teaching
The assemblage of the saintly will be my sanctuary.

All our learning and thinking
All prayers and penances
Are directed to God who is beyond comprehension
    and whose secret is unravelled.
Sayeth Nanak, my mind is imbued with the Name of
    Rama,
Teaching of the guru hath pointed out to me the gentle
    path of *sahaj* and service.

* * *

Vidya vichari tan parupkari

If you desire to acquire true knowledge
Make people's welfare thy aim in life.
When you master your five senses
Life itself will become a pilgrimage.
When the mind is stilled
It hears the tinkle of a dancer's bells.
What then can Yama do to thee?
He who abandons desires,
Is the real sanyasi.
He who has mastered passions
Enjoys his body and is a true yogi.
He who has compassion
And looks within himself
Is like a sky-clad Digambar hermit.
For he has killed his self without killing anyone.

O Nanak, he who knows Thy sportive ways
Knows Thou art One but hath many disguises.

* * *

Tit sarvade bhai lai nivasa

We live in a pond whose waters
He Himself hath filled with fire;
Our feet are stuck in the mud of attachment
We cannot move; many have I seen sunk in the mire.

Heart! Foolish heart! Never dwellest thou on the One
If thou forgettest thy Lord,
Thou shalt dissipate the deserts of the virtue.
Neither continent, nor truthful, nor learned am I,
Foolish and ignorant was I begot;
Nanak prays for the protection of those
Who never have Thine Name forgot.

* * *

Deeva mera ek nam dukh vich paya tel

The Name of the Lord is my only lamp
In it I put my sorrows of oil;
The brighter burns the flame
The quicker is consumed the oil
Thus I escape encounter with the demon of death.

People, do not mock me!
Just as a thousand piles of logs
Can be lit by a tiny spark
(So can the Name set alight the world).

(For my obsequial ceremony)
Instead of rice-cakes and leaf-plates
Be used the Name of God.
The Name of the True Creator shall also my oblations be,
In this world and the worlds to come
In the future and in time past

He alone hath been my refuge.
Lord, Thy praise will be my pilgrimage to Benares
My soul will dip into the waters of the holy Ganga
My ablution will be performed if day and night I
    cherish Thee.
Some rice-cakes are offered to the ancestors,
Others to the spirits that wander round the globe;
But it is the Brahmins who eat them all.
O Nanak, if there is grace upon the rice-cake
Never never will it go to waste.

* * *

Man maigal sakat devana, ban khand maya moh hairana

Our mind is like a rogue elephant crazed with notions
    of its own might.
It lives in a jungle of delusions and attachment.
It runs hither and thither in terror of death
If it finds the guru to guide, it will find its sanctuary.

Without the guru's word, the mind will not be stilled;
Repeat the Name of Rama, it is utterly pure
Abandon other ritual, it is bitterness of the ego.

How can this wayward mind be stilled?
Unless it understands, it will suffer at the hands of death.
God is our Saviour,
The true guru can unite us with God.

He can draw the thorn of death out of our flesh
He can make truth triumphant.
The mind though compounded of five elements
Determines our destiny for it is the doer
And in the mind is law divine.
The mind of the fool worships power and is full of greed,
By the guru's advice it worships the Name, is freed
And attains eternal felicity.

Under the guru's instruction the mind finds its true
    function;
Under the guru's instruction the mind comprehends
    the three worlds.
The mind can be a celibate yogi or the householder.
The mind can be a performer of penances;
Under the guru's instruction it can realize God.

Thus doth the restless mind come to rest
And relinquish thoughts of self.
In every heart is the contagion of duality;
Under instruction of the guru (it avoids the contagion)
It tastes the divine essence of God.
And at every door of every home and mansion it is
    welcomed with honour.
This mind of ours can be a monarch
And the hero of the field of battle,
The guru gives it the gift of the Name and makes it
    fearless.

Man, conquer your five enemies
(lust, anger, greed, attachment and pride)
Reduce them to servitude
And along with your ego bundle them into one!

The music of the guru's message fulfils
Man loses taste for other food.
The guru's message awakens the mind to worship.
It hears music unstruck and meditates on the Name
It understands its spiritual self and becomes formless.

In the mansion of the Lord is our mind purified
The guru teaches it to love and worship.
Day and night it sings praises of God—such grace the
    guru brings
In every heart is God who is without end and without
    a beginning.

This mind is drunk with juices of God
Under the guru's instruction find God, the curer of all
    ailments.
Sit at the feet of the guru and become a worshipper
Nanak is the slave of the slaves of the people of God.

* * *

Roodo Thakur mahro roodi Gurbani

Excellent is my Master,

Excellent are the songs of the guru,
The very fortunate meet the true guru
And attain salvation.

I am lowest of the low,
I am Thy slave boy,
As Thou keepest so shall I live.
Thy name will ever be on my lips.

I thirst for vision of Thee
Thy ordinances my heart accepts
My Master holds greatness in the palm of His hand
If it be His pleasure, I will be received with honour.

Do not regard the True One as far away,
He is within us.
Whichever way I turn, I see Him there;
Who has evaluated Him?

He makes, He demolishes,
He watches and glories in His work.
By treading the saintly path
We shall have His vision
And thus appraise His worth.

Such are the doings of the guru
That in this life we can earn profit.
But we can only find the true guru
If it is writ in our book of fate.

The perverse of mind will forever suffer loss
They stumble in superstition and mislead others
The perverse of mind are like the blind.
If they recall Him not to their mind,
How can they expect to see Him?
When you have attached yourself to the True One
Consider your lives on earth worthwhile;
The guru is like a touchstone
On meeting him (iron is transmuted into gold)
He blends your light with the Light Eternal.

Ever and always remain aloof from things of the world
Serve only the Primal Lord.
Sayeth Nanak, the name produces tranquillity
It absorbs us in love of the feet of God.

* * *

Toon sun harna kalia kee vadeeai rata Ram

Black buck, listen to me!
What makes thee break into fenced-off fields?
Forbidden fruit tastes sweet but for four short days
Thereafter it produces ill-humours in the body.
What thou cravest produces great sorrow and anguish.
Those who forego the Name
Suffer the flames of hell.
As short-lived as the wave in the ocean,

Brief as the flash of lightning,
Is the joy of forbidden fruit.
There is no other protector save God.
And it is God thou hast forsaken.
Sayeth Nanak, man ponder over this in thy heart:
What is it that makes the black buck race to its doom?
O Rama! My mind is like the honey bee
(Stealing nectar from the flowers);
O Rama! It will suffer great affliction.
I asked my guru about bees and creepers in bloom.
The guru pondered and asked me in return
'Why like the honey bee art thou lost amongst the
    flowers?'
When (ends the night of life and) the sun riseth,
With hot oil will your body be scalded.
You will be in the thrall of death,
Buffeted by Yama's blows;
Without the Word, you will be like an evil spirit.'

'O my soul!' says Nanak truthfully, 'meditate on the
    Lord
For the way of the black honey bee is the way to
    damnation.'
My soul! thou art not native to this world.
Why dost thou enmesh thyself in it?
If the True Master dwell in thy heart
How can the noose of Yama fall on thee?

As when the fisherman separates the fish from the
    water
And puts it in his net
The fishes' eyes fill with tears
(So will it be with thee).
The world which we cherish as sweet
Is but a delusion.
Only in the end is the veil of delusion
Lifted from our eyes.
Fix your mind on God
Free it of anxieties.
Nanak speaks the truth:
My soul, ponder over the fact that
Thou art not native to this world.

O Rama! Rivers in their course break into streams
And streams again run back into the river,
So are our souls united with God from whom they came.
O Rama! Some rare one who hath renounced the world
    knows
That the world which appears so sweet in every age
Is really full of venom.
Those who meditate on the message of the true guru
Find Truth through the gentle way of *sahaj*
And realize God.
Without the Name of God thoughtless fools are we;
We stumble on paths of ignorance and superstition.

Those who worship not the Name of Hari
Nor have truth in their hearts
Will regret it in the end; they'll beat their breasts and
    lament.
Nanak speaks the truth when he says
Through the Word we meet the Truth
And our prolonged separation ends in ultimate union.

* * *

Purkhan birkhan teerthan tattan meghan khetan

Mankind and arbours
Places of pilgrimage by river banks
Clouds that float over farmers' fields
Islands and spheres,
Continents and the universe, the entire cosmos.

All that is born of egg and womb,
Born of water and sweat
Of all these He alone hath estimate.

O Nanak, He knows the oceans and the mountains
He knows the masses of mankind
O Nanak, He who gave life to creatures
He will keep them in His mind.

He who makes must take care of what He hath made!
Let the cares of the world He made be His worry.

To Him make obeisance, to Him be victory!
May His court be in eternal session!
O Nanak, if we have not the True Name
Worthless is the mark on the forehead,
Worthless too the sacred thread.

* * *

Sach to par janeeai ja ridai sacha hoi

He alone is truly truthful
In whose heart is the True One living
Whose soul within is rinsed of falsehood
And his body without is cleansed by washing.

He alone is truly truthful
Who loves truth with passion
Whose heart rejoices in the Name
And finds the door to salvation.

He alone is truly truthful
Who knows the art of living
Who prepares his body like a bed
And plants the seed of the Lord therein.

He alone is truly truthful
Who accepts the true message
Towards the living shows mercy
Gives something as alms and in charity.

He alone is truly truthful
Whose soul in pilgrimage resides
Who consults the true guru
And by his counsel ever abides.

Truth is the nostrum for all ills.
It exorcizes sin, washes the body clean.
Those that have truth in their aprons
Before them doth Nanak himself demean.

* * *

Simal rukh saradya ati diragh ati much

The *simal* tree is huge and straight
But if one comes to it with hope of gain
What will one get and whither turn?
Its fruit is without taste
Its flowers have no fragrance
Its leaves are of no use.
O Nanak, humility and sweetness
Are the essence of virtue and goodness.
Readily do we all pay homage to ourselves
Before others we refuse to bow.

Weigh anything in a pair of scales and see
That of greater substance does the lower go.
The wicked man bends over double
As deer-slayer shooting his dart.

What use is bending or bowing of head
When you bow not your heart?

* * *

Daya kapah santokh soot jat gandhi sat vat

When making the sacred thread, the *Janeau*,
See that following rules you pursue.
Out of the cotton of compassion
Spin the thread of tranquillity
Let continence be the knot
And virtue the twist thereon.
O pandit, if such a sacred thread there be
Around our neck, we shall wear it willingly.

A thread so made will not break
It will not get dirty, be burnt or lost.
O Nanak, thou shall see
Those who wear this shall blessed be.

For four cowrie shells this thread is bought
A square is marked for the ceremony.
The Brahmin whispers a *mantra* in the ear
And thus becomes the guru and teacher.
But when the wearer dies, cast away is his thread
And threadless he goes on his voyage ahead.

* * *

Je kar sootak manneeai sab tai sootak hoe

Once we say: This is pure, this unclean,
See that in all things there is life unseen.
There are worms in wood and cowdung cakes,
There is life in the corn ground into bread.
There is life in the water which turns plants green.
How then be clean when impurity is over the kitchen
    spread?

O Nanak, not thus are things impure purified
Wash them with divine knowledge instead.
Impurity of the mind is greed,
Of tongue, untruth
Impurity of the eye is coveting
Another's wealth, his wife, her comeliness;
Impurity of the ears is listening to calumny.
O Nanak, thus does the fettered soul
Wing its way to the city of doom.

* * *

Apey bhandey sajeean apey pooran dey

God gives shape to human vessels
And God fills them with what He wills
Into some He pours milk
Others He makes simmer on the hearths,
Some are destined to sleep on soft couches

Others spend their nights keeping a vigil,
He saves those whom He wills.

* * *

Vade kiyan vadieyeean

Beyond speech is the glory of the Great One
He is the Creator, mighty and benign.
To each He gives his living
Our lives fulfil His great design.
God is our one and only refuge
Besides Him there is no second one
Whatever pleases Him, He causes to be done.

* * *

Tera nam karee channatheea jey man ursa hoe

If our minds could be made into grindstones,
Thy Name the stick of sandal to rub upon them;
If our good deeds could be as saffron
(And with paste so made we anointed our gods)
That worship would be worship from the heart.

Let our worship be meditation on Thy Name;
Without the Name there is no worship.
We bathe our gods; why not bathe our minds?
Why not rinse our hearts of lies

And thus take the road to paradise?
Learn goodness from your cattle!
You give them only hay
With nectar-like milk they repay.
But man is ungrateful,
He forgets the Name.
(He gives no thanks to his Maker)
Accursed is his life and all he does.

The Lord is beside you,
Deem Him not far away.
Forever He watches over us
And cares for us.
Sayeth Nanak, whatever He gives we eat
That is the Truth
(That Truth is sweet).

* * *

*Kavan kavan jachah Prabhu datey takey ant na
  parah sumar*

There is no limit to Thy bounty,
There is no count of those who beg of Thee,
Thou art most bountiful.
Whatever be the hunger in the heart
Dost Thou fulfil it: Thou art Truth Omnipotent
Thou art the Great Giver.

Ho Sir! Prayer, penance and control of the senses
Need to be supported by Truth.
If God grants us the gift of the Name
We attain peace.
Thy treasure is brimful with devotion.

Many are entranced in profound meditation
They concentrate only on the one divine Word;
They are not aware of water nor of land,
Neither of the earth nor of the sky;
They are conscious only of the Creator who made
    them all.
Not for them is maya's cup of delusion
For them ignorance casts no shade
They are not bothered by the eternal light of the sun or
    the moon.
They comprehend entire creation in the heart's eye
And in one glance take in the three worlds.

They know that God made air, water and fire;
God made Brahma, Vishnu and Siva;
We all are but beggars at Thy door
Thou alone art our Lord, the Great Giver.
Thou givest us gifts as it pleases Thee.

Thirty-three million gods beg of Thee;
Thou givest, but Thy store never diminishes.
A vessel held upside down can contain nothing

Placed as it should be it can be filled with ambrosia.
Miracle-makers in trance know Thee in their hearts
They beg miracles from Thee
And cry 'To Thee be victory!'
Whatever the mind thirsts for
He slakes that thirst.

Great is the fortune of those who can serve their guru
From them there are no secrets separating guru from
    God.
For them there is no death nor fear of death,
They know the Word and in their hearts meditate
    thereon.

Neither now nor at any later time
Shall I ask God for anything besides the Name;
(The Name) unsullied and Love Divine.
As the *Chatrik* bird (craves for drops of rain)
So shall Nanak crave for drops of nectar.
Merciful Lord, we shall our voices raise
Give us the power to sing Thy praise.

* * *

Amli amal na ambdai machi neer na hoe

To the opium addict there is nothing like opium.
To the fish water is everything.

Those imbued with the Name of their Lord
Find every prospect pleasing.

May every moment of my life be a sacrifice to Thy
   Name, O my Master!

My Master is like a tree that beareth fruit
The Name of the fruit is nectar
Those who drink its juice are truly fulfilled
May my life be sacrificed to them!

Thou livest amongst all creatures
Yet I see Thee not;
How can the thirsty their thirst slake,
If a wall separates them from the like?

Nanak is Thy tradesman;
Thou art my Master and my goods.
My mind would rid itself of delusion
If to Thee I addressed my prayers
And to Thee my petition.

* * *

Mori run jhun laya, bhainey savan aya

Sweet sound of water gurgling down the water-spout
(The peacock's shrill, exultant cry)
Sister, it's *savan*, the month of rain!

Beloved Thine eyes bind me in a spell
(They pierce through me like daggers)
They fill my heart with greed and longing;
For one glimpse of Thee I'll give my life
For Thy Name may I be a sacrifice.
When Thou art mine, my heart fills with pride,
What can I be proud of if Thou art not with me?
Woman, smash thy bangles on thy bedstead

Break thy arms, break the arms of thy couch;
Thy adornments hold no charms
Thy Lord is in another's arms.

The Lord liked not thy bangle-seller
Thy bracelets and glass bangles He doth spurn
Arms that do not the Lord's neck embrace
With anguish shall forever burn.
All my friends have gone to their lovers
I feel wretched, whose door shall I seek?
Friends, of proven virtue and fair am I
Lord, does nothing about me find favour in Thine eye?

I plaited my tresses,
With vermilion daubed the parting of my hair
And went to Him
But with me He would not lie.
My heart is grief-stricken, I could die.
I wept, and the world wept with me.

Even birds of the forest cried,
Only my soul torn out of my body shed not a tear,
Nay, my soul which separated me from my Beloved
    shed not a tear.
In a dream He came to me
(I woke) and He was gone.
I wept a flood of tears.
Beloved I cannot come to Thee,
No messenger will take my message;
Blessed sleep come thou back to me,
That in my dreams my Lover I again may see!
Nanak, what wilt thou give the messenger
Who brings thee a message from thy Master?
I'll sever my head to make a seat for him;
Headless though I be, I'll continue to serve him.
Why then do I not die? Why not give away my life?
My Husband is estranged from me and has taken
    another wife!

* * *

Jalao aisee reet jit mai pyara veesrai

Ritual that makes me forget my Beloved Lord shall I
    burn.
O Nanak that love is best that in the Lord's eyes doth
    merit earn.
The body is like a wife in her home,

When her Lord is away
She pines for him.
If her intentions are pure, she'll be reunited any time
    any day.

O Nanak, unless there be love,
False and futile is all talk.
Man who calculates good
In the spirit of give and take
Even for the good he does
He doth its virtue vitiate.

* * *

Sabhna marna dya vichhoda sabhna

Death will come to everyone,
To everyone separation,
Who will heareafter be reunited?
Go ask the wise ones.
Those who forget my Master
Will suffer much tribulation.

Forever worship Him who is the Truth
By His grace you will gain joy everlasting.

Praise Him as the Mighty
He alone is and ever shall be.
Lord, Thou art the One, the Only Giver;

Mankind's gifts account for nothing.
What Thou ordainest comes to pass
All else is as futile as women's wailing.

Many raised forts and castles upon the earth
Proclaimed dominion by beat of drum—and passed on;
Those who walked with their heads in the clouds
Are now like beasts led by the nose-string.

Man knowing how like a stake driven through the body
Will be thy pain
Thou eatest sweet things of the world,
Why dost thou not abstain?

Sayeth Nanak, the more we sin, the heavier the chain
    we forge about our necks.
It can be severed by good deeds which are like our
    brothers and well-wishers.
When we pass on and our credentials are examined
Those who had no guru are beaten and discarded.

* * *

Alakh apar agam agochar na tis kal na karma

Beyond comprehension, without end
Beyond reach, beyond description
Immortal, beyond cause and effect
Beyond the pale of caste and castelessness

Beyond the cycle of life, death and rebirth
Self-existent and alone
Without desire, without delusion.

He is the Truest of the True
To Him I sacrifice my life.

He hath no form nor colour nor line
He manifests Himself through His Word divine.

He hath no mother or father or other kin
He hath no woman nor lusts for one;
He hath no forefathers, nothing contaminates Him,
He is endless, He is infinite.

Thou art the light of all light.
In every heart art Thou hid
In every heart burneth Thy light.
The guru's message bursts open the granite doors to
    understanding
And it reveals the Fearless One entranced in profound
    meditation.

He created life and over it spread the pall of death
All man's cunning devices He knows and controls.
Serve the true guru, a priceless treasure will be thine.
To gain release, live according to the Word divine.

If thy vessel (thy body) be clean, the True One will
    enter it and there remain;
But rare are those whose character is without stain.
As essences merge in the quintessence
So doth man's soul blend in the primal soul.
Sayeth Nanak, Lord, Thou art my refuge.

* * *

Jis jal nidhi karan tum jag aye so amrit gur pahi jeeo

The elixir you came into the world to seek
That sacred font of nectar you'll find with the guru;
Take off your mask and other disguises
Give up trickery and all other pursuit
Doubt and duality bear no fruit.
Man, stand firm, go not astray
If elsewhere you look, yours will be frustration and grief
For the ambrosia you seek
Is within your heart, within your home.

Abandon the path of evil, take the path of virtue
You'll regret the evil acts you do.
If you know not good from evil, (the further you go)
The deeper in the mire will you sink.

Of what avail is external washing of the body,
When the grime of greed and falsehood is within?

If under the guru's guidance you worship the pure
    Name
You will be saved, your inner self be cleansed of sin.

Discard greed and calumny, with falsehood make no
    compromise
With the guru's teaching pluck the fruit of truth.
As be Thy will, O Lord,
So keep me, I crave.
Praises of Thy Word I'll sing,
Nanak is Thy bond slave.

* * *

Jeeo darat hai apna kai seo karee pukar

My mind is beset with fears
Before whom shall I cry for help?
I shall serve the Remover of Sorrows
He is forever bountiful, He gives me what I ask.

My Master reveals Himself,
Ever fresh, forever new,
He is forever and ever bountiful.

Night and day will I serve my Master
When comes my end, He will be my Redeemer.

Woman who has bewitched my heart, O hark! O hear!
The Lord alone can take us to the other shore.

O Merciful Lord, Thy Name shall be my boat.
To Thee shall I sacrifice my life forever.
In all the world Thou alone art True
There is none besides Thee
On whom falls Thy grace,
Are destined to serve Thee.

Beloved, without Thee how shall I survive?
Grant me the boon that I cling to Thy Name.
My Love, there is no other to whom I can turn.

Master, Thee alone shall I serve, of Thee alone will I beg;
Forever will Nanak be Thy servant.
Every joint and limb of my body I dedicate to Him,
Yea, every limb and every joint I offer to my Master.

* * *

Jeeo tapat hai baro bar

Fires of temptation assail me time and again,
I weaken and am a prey to many ills;
I forgot the guru's hymns
And like one chronically sick and in bodily pain
I groan and moan and complain.

Too much talk is foolish prattle
Without our telling

He knows everything
That is worth knowing.

He who gave us ears, eyes and nose,
Who gave us tongue so cunning of speech,
He who preserved us in the furnace of the womb
At His bidding is all the breath we breathe.

As strong our attachments, our loves and cravings
So black is the stain they leave on our reputations.
Those who pursue the path of transgression will be
   branded
And will not find a seat in His presence.

By Thy grace we have power to worship Thy Name
Thy Name alone saves, we have no other recourse.
Even those sunk can thus be salvaged
O Nanak, the True One is bounteous towards everyone.

* * *

*Chor salahai cheet na bheejai, jey badi karai ta
   tasoo na chheejai*

Words of praise from a thief do not please the mind
Nor words of calumny spoken by him in the least
   detract;
For a thief no one stands surety, no one will hold a brief
How can anything good be expected of a thief?

My mind, listen! Thou blind, base cur! listen forsooth
Without being told, the True One finds the Truth.

A thief may appear learned and wise
He'll be a base coin worth two pies
However much you mix the base with the genuine
Base will be found to be base when carefully examined.

As our acts, so will our deserts be
As we sow, so shall we reap;
Of himself whatever a man may say
(It changes not his real self) his senses determine his way.

A hundred lies he may tell to cover up his filth and
    falsehood;
He may win acclaim all over the world.
(It will not help, the base can never be good)
If it be Thy will, even a fool wilt Thou receive
O Nanak, He is wise and omniscient,
Nobody doth the Lord deceive.

* * *

ARTI: Gagan mai thal ravi chand dipak banai

The firmament is Thy salver
The sun and moon Thy lamps;
The galaxy of stars as pearls strewn.
A mountain of sandal is Thy joss-stick

Breezes that blow Thy fan;
All the woods and vegetation
All flowers that bloom
Take their colours from Thy light.

Thus we wave the salver of lamps
How beautiful is this ritual!
Thou art the destroyer of the cycle of birth, death and
    rebirth.
In Thy temple echo beats the drum unstruck by hands.

A thousand eyes hast Thou, yet no eye hast Thou.
A thousand shapes hast Thou, yet no shape hast Thou.
A thousand feet hast Thou, yet no foot hast Thou.
A thousand nostrils hast Thou, yet no nose hast Thou.
These are miracles that have bewitched my heart.

Thine is the light in every lamp.
Thine the radiance in all that is radiant.
The guru's teaching illumines our minds.
What pleases Him is the true worship of lamps.

As the honey bee seeks honey in flowers
My soul which is ever athirst,
Seeks Thy lotus feet
To slake its thirst for nectar.

Lord, show Thy mercy

Give Nanak the water he seeks.
He like the sarang cries for rain
Let him forever abide in Thy Name.

* * *

Gur sagar ratani bharpoorey

The guru is a sea full of pearls
The saintly are like swans that feed
And are never far from its shore.
They pick up their share of the nectar (of the Name)
The Lord loves them and holds them dear.
In this sea the swans find God, the Lord of life.

The wretched heron wades in the dirty pond
It wallows in the mire, it cannot be cleansed.
The wise watch their steps ere they go
They reject duality and worship God as the Formless
    One.
They drink nectar and attain salvation
The guru rescues them from the cycle of death and
    rebirth.

Swans never leave the sea,
With love and adoration they gently become a part of it.
Then is the swan in the sea and the sea within the swan
It knows the unknowable and pays homage to the
    guru's words.

Entranced in profound meditation is the Divine Yogi
He is neither male nor female, how can one describe Him?
In the three worlds is His divine light worshipped
Gods and men and ascetics seek refuge in Him.

God is the root of the tree of bliss,
He is the Protector of the helpless;
In meditation and in worship
Men of God follow the gentle method of *sahaj*.
God cherishes His worshippers, He is the Destroyer
    of fear
Man conquers his ego, his steps turn towards the Lord.

Man tries countless other devices but death dogs his
    footsteps;
For those who came into the world, death is destined
Life is an invaluable gift, man squanders it in duality,
He knows it not himself, he stumbles in doubt and
    sorely grieves.

Those who know speak, read, and hear praises of the
    One God,
The God who supports the earth,
He instils in them faith and fortitude, and becomes
    their protector.
Their minds become chaste, righteous and self-
    controlled
If they choose, they attain the fourth estate.

So pure are the truthful, nothing can soil them;
The guru's teaching dispels doubt and fear.
Nanak begs of the Truthful One, the Primal Lord
Handsome of face and feature which are beyond compare.

* * *

Teerath navan jao teerath Nam hai

Why go ye on pilgrimage to bathe in holy waters?
Know that real pilgrimage is worship of the Name!
True pilgrimage is meditation on the Word and
    knowledge of the self.
Knowledge imparted by the guru is more real (than a
    sacred river bank);
It is more rewarding than bathing on the ten holy days;

It is like an unending festival of Dussehra.
Forever shall I beg the Name of God, Hari.
God, Sustainer of the world, give Thy Name to me!
The world is sick, God's Name is the remedy.
If we do not have the Name of the True One
We shall forever be smeared in sin.
The guru's teaching is pure, eternally effulgent.
It is ever the truest pilgrimage and ablution.

Dirt does not stick to those who are truthful
They have no need to scrub or rinse themselves.

If you string a garland of good deeds around your neck,
You need not then raise cries of regret.
Contemplation conquers ego,
It helps man save himself and save others.
It prevents rebirth.

The one who contemplates becomes the supreme
  meditator.
The touchstone (whereby all truths are tested)
The truthful please the Truthful One.

Day and night is he in true ecstatic bliss
Sin and sorrow do not afflict him.
He hath found the Name of the True One.
The guru hath shown him the way to God.
No sin can stain him because
The True One abides in his heart.

Meeting and companionship of the men of God is real
  bathing, true pilgrimage,
One who sings the songs of the Lord is himself exalted,
Praise the True One, have faith in the true guru.
Thy nature will turn to giving alms and charity,
Performing of good deeds and acts of mercy.
If thou love being with thy Lord
In the gentle stream of *sahaj* willst thou then bathe
It is a stream as holy as the *Sangam*
(Where meet Ganga, Yamuna and Saraswati).

Thou shalt be the truest of the true;
Thou shalt worship the One God who is the truth
And whose bounty ever increaseth.
Friends! Company of the saintly
Is the way to salvation.
God grants this in His grace and unites us with Himself.

Everyone speaks of the Lord
Who can say how great He is?
I am foolish, low-born and ignorant
I learn from the guru's teaching
Which is like drinking pure nectar.

It persuaded my mind to accept the truth.
We come into the world with a load of sin,
We depart with the self-same load.
Only my guru's teaching explains the truth to me.
We can endlessly talk of the Lord; He Himself is the
    keeper of the treasure of worship.
His presence is felt everywhere.
Nanak speaks the truth and pleads
He who cleanses his heart is truly cleansed.

* * *

Yak arj guftam pes to dar gos kun kartar

Creator! A petition I place at Thy door
Give ear and hear what I have to say.

Thou art just, great, merciful and of evil free
Thou art Protector of all things that be.

We must always bear in mind
That the world is perishable.
The angel of death hath my hair in his grasp
And yet my heart hath no knowledge of it.

Neither wife nor son, neither father nor brother,
Not one can extend to me a helping hand!
When comes my time to depart,
Time to say the final prayer
No one will hear my call,
And to my rescue come.

Night and day, I trod the path of greed
My mind thought only evil thoughts
I did not do any good deed.

I am unfortunate, niggardly and thoughtless,
A shameless wretch am I;
I have even lost the fear of God.
Sayeth Nanak, Thy slave am I,
Yea, I am the dust of the feet of Thy slaves.

* * *

Guru Nanak

Ih tan maya pahia pyarey leetda lab rangae

Dear friend, I am like one drowned in a dyer's vat
Brimful with delusions of maya
I have become like a cloth dyed with greed.
Dear friend, the colour of my cloak
Pleases not the Lord my Groom.
How then shall I who am His bride,
Be invited to His nuptial couch?

Let my life be a sacrifice unto Thee, O Merciful One!
Let my life be a sacrifice!
Let my life be a sacrifice to those who worship Thy
    Name.
Yea, let my life be sacrificed to them a hundred
    times.

Dear friend, if the body be like a dyer's vat
We must fill it with the madder of the Lord's Name;
The Divine Dyer will dye it in hues none hath ever
    seen.

Dear friend, she whose garment is thus dyed
Hath the Lord her Groom by her side.
Nanak prays for the dust of her feet.

The Lord weaves the cloth and dyes it.
He Himself appraises the colours.

Sayeth Nanak, if the woman thus adorned please Him
He will be gracious and take her unto Himself.

* * *

Jog na khintha, jog na dandey, jog na bhasam chadhaeeai

Religion lieth not in the patched coat the yogi wears,
Not in the staff he bears,
Nor in the ashes on his body.
Religion lieth not in rings in the ears,
Not in a shaven head,
Nor in the blowing of the conch-shell.
If thou must the path of true religion see,
Among the world's impurities, be of impurities free.

Not by talk can you achieve union
He who sees all mankind as equals
Can be deemed to be a yogi.

Religion lieth not in visiting tombs
Nor in visiting places where they burn the dead
Not in sitting entranced in contemplation
Nor in wandering in the countryside or foreign lands
Nor in bathing at places of pilgrimage.
If thou must the path of true religion see,
Among the world's impurities, be of impurities free.

When a man meets the true guru
His doubts are dispelled
And his mind ceases its wanderings;
Drops of nectar pour down on him like rain.
His ears catch strains of *sahaj's* celestial music
And his mind is lit up with knowledge divine.
If thou must the path of true religion see,
Among the world's impurities, be of impurities free.

Sayeth Nanak, if thou must be a real yogi,
Be in the world but be dead to its tinsel values.
When the lute strikes notes without being touched
Know then that thou hast conquered fear.
If thou must the path of true religion see,
Among the world's impurities, be of impurities free.

* * *

Sabh avgun mai gun nahi koe

Full of evil, no virtues have I
How will I my husband meet?
My face is not comely, there is no lustre in my eyes
I have no lineage, no winsome ways, nor sweet speech.

She who comes adorned with the beauty nature gave
Shall find favour with her Lord
And her marriage consummated.

He hath neither form nor shape
But seek Him now.
Put of not prayer till the end is near.
I have no sense, no learning, no ability
Lord have mercy, let me clasp Thy feet.
What avail is my youth
If it please not my Lord?
Maya hath deluded me; I have lost my way.
When the notion of self goes, God enters
Then the bride finds her Groom and the nine treasures.
Many lives have I spent sorrowing separated from Thee
My Lord, my lover take me in Thine arms and save me
Says Nanak: those He likes, He accepts
The Lord is—and ever shall be.

* * *

Sau ulame dinai key rati milan sahans

The day's hundred regrets
By night multiply tenfold;
As a swan instead of feeding on pearls
(Which are the real sustenance)
Pecks at carrion
So man forgets to sing hosannas to his God
(Which are the real sustenance for his soul
And turns instead to the fleshpots of the world).

Cursed be the life thus wasted
In stuffing food and increasing the paunch.
The Name of the True One changes not; that much we
    know
All else, sayeth Nanak, turns from friend to foe.

* * *

Deeva balai andhera jai, bed path mati papa khai

When a lamp is lit, darkness is dispelled
Where scriptures are read, evil thoughts are expelled.
When the sun rises, the moon is not seen
When knowledge comes, ignorance is dispelled.
The reading of the Vedas is now a worldly trade
O pandit! You read much, but without thought,
Without understanding this reading is a loss.
Says Nanak, only those the guru loves will go across.

* * *

Too sultan kaha hau miyan teri kavan vaddiaee

Thou art the Sultan
If I address Thee as the village headman
Do I magnify Thy Name?
Lord, I address thee as Thou hast empowered me
I am foolish and know not the art of polite speech.

As Thou instructest me so shall I word my praise
Thy will shall be my way of life, in Thy truth shall I
    abide.

All that comes to pass is at Thy bidding
Everything that happens is within Thy knowing
My Master, I know not Thy dimensions
I have no means of knowing, I am blind.

What shall I say? I tried to speak
I learned that I could not speak of One
Who is beyond description.
I can only say as much as Thou willst me to say
And that is but a tiny fragment of Thy real greatness.
You are the shade in which we rest
And the mansions we raise.

None other besides You will I ever know, O Master,
Forever shall I sing in praise of You.

Men and beasts, all Your shelter seek
You have to look after everyone.
This is Nanak's one prayer and only request
That he look upon Your will as the best.

* * *

BARA MAHA OR THE TWELVE MONTHS

(The practise of composing lyrics according to the twelve months of the year, to highlight human emotions and make spiritual or moral messages accessible to people, was common among Indian poets. Guru Nanak's Barah Mah, *composed in Tukhari raga, is the most highly rated in the Punjabi language. It is believed to be among the last of the Guru's compositions.)*

Chet (March-April)

Chet basant bhala bhavar suhavre

It is the month of Chet,
It is spring. All is seemly—
The humming bumble-bee
And the woodland in flower—
But there is a sorrow in my soul.

The Lord, my Master is away.
If the Husband comes not home, how can a wife
Find peace of mind?

Sorrows of separation waste away the body.
The *Koil* calls in the mango grove,
Its notes are full of joy.
Why then the sorrow in my soul?

The bumble-bee hovers about the blossoming bough,
O mother of mine, it is like death to me,
For there is a sorrow in my soul.

Nanak says: When the Lord her Master comes home
to her,
Blessed is then the month of Chet.

Vaisakh (April-May)

Vaisakh bhala sakha ves kare

In beauteous Vaisakh the bough adorns itself anew,
The wife awaits the coming of her Lord,
Her eyes fixed on the door.
'My Love, You alone can help me across
The turbulent waters of life. Come home.
Without You I am worthless as a broken shell.
When You look upon me with favour, Love,
And our eyes mingle;
Then shall I become priceless beyond compare.'

Nanak says: 'Where seek you the Lord?
Whom are you awaiting?
You have not far to go to find Him.
He is within you, you are His mansion.
If your body and soul yearn for the Lord,
The Lord shall love you and Vaisakh be beautiful.'

Jeth *(May-June)*

Mah jeth bhala pritam kiun bisrai

Why forget the Beloved in the month of Jeth
When the land shimmers in the summer's heat?
Grant me the Virtues, O Lord,
As win favour in Your eyes.
You are free from all attachment
And live in Truth.
And I am lowly, humble, helpless.
How shall I approach You?
How find the haven of peace?

Says Nanak: She who knows the Lord
Becomes like the Lord.
She knows Him
By treading the path of virtue.

Asad *(June-July)*

Asad bhala suraj gagan tape

In Asad the Sun scorches.
The sky is hot
The earth burns like an oven,
Waters give up their vapours.
It burns and scorches relentlessly in the month of Asad.

The Sun's chariot passes the noon's sky
The wife watches the shadow creep across the courtyard.
And the cicada calls from the glades.
The beloved seeks the cool of the evening.
If the comfort she seeks be in falsehood,
There will be sorrow in store for her.
If it be in truth,
Hers will be a life of joy.

Says Nanak: Life and life's end are at the will of
                    the Lord
                    To Him have I surrendered my soul.

Savan (July-August)

Savan sars mana ghan varsai

The season of rain has come.
My heart is full of joy,
My body and soul yearn for the Master.
But He is away in foreign lands
If He return not, I shall die pining for Him.

The lightning strikes terror in my heart.
I am alone in my courtyard
In solitude and sorrow.

O Mother of mine, I stand on the brink of death,
Without the Lord I have no hunger nor sleep
I cannot suffer the clothes on my body.

Nanak says: She alone is blest
           Who becomes One with the Lord.

Bhadon *(August-September)*

Bhadon bharm bhuli bhar joban pachtani

Lost in the maze of falsehood
I waste my full-bloom youth.
River and land are one expanse of water
For it is the glad season of the rains.
It rains.
The nights are dark.
There is no peace for me.
Frogs croak in contentment.
Peacocks cry with joy.
The *papeeha* calls peeooh, peeooh.
The fangs of serpents that crawl,
The bite of mosquitoes that fly,
Are full of venom.

The seas have burst their bounds in the ecstasy
    of fulfilment.
I alone am bereft of joy,

Whither shall I go?
How shall I find Him?

Nanak says: Ask of the Guru the way
               He knows the path which leads to the
                   Lord.

Asan (September-October)

Asun au pira sadhan jhur mui

O Master come to me,
I waste and will die.
If the Master wills,
I shall meet Him.
If He wills not,
I am lost utterly.
I took the path of falsehood,
And the Master forsook me,
Age has greyed my locks
I have lived many winters
The fires of hell still lie ahead,
And I am afraid.

The bough remains ever green
For the sap that moves within
Night and day, renews life.

If the Name of the Lord courses in your veins,
Life and hope will for ever be green.
Meditate calmly on the Name.
That which ripens slowly ripens best.

Nanak says: Come now, my Love,
                Even the Guru pleads for me.

Katak (October-November)

Katak kirat paiya jo prabh bhae

What pleases the Lord
Is all I merit.
The lamp of wisdom burns steadily
If the oil that feeds it
Be reality.
If the oil that feeds the lamp be Love
The beloved will meet the Lord and find fulfilment.

Full of faults, she is caught
In the cycle of birth and death
And finds no favour with the Lord.
Good deeds alone will end her sorrow.

Those who are granted the worship of Your Name
Hope to meet You in Your mansion.

Nanak says: O Lord till You grant us Your vision
               And break the bonds of superstition,
               One watch of day will drag like half
               a year.

Maghar (November-December)

Maghar mah bhala harigun ank smavai

The month of Maghar is bliss
To her who is lost in the Lord
For she is the virtuous one
And loves the Lord Eternal.

He Who is eternal, omniscient, wise is also the Master
    of destiny.
The world is in turmoil without faith.
She who has knowledge and contemplates on Him
Loses herself in Him.
By His grace she loves the Lord.

Proclaim the name of Rama in song and dance and verse,
And sorrow will flee away.

Nanak says: Only she is loved
               Who prays to her Lord
               With her heart.

Pokh (December-January)

Pokh tukhar pare van trin ras sokhai

As the winter snow
Freezes the sap in tree and bush,
The absence of the Lord
Blights the body and the soul.
O Lord why do You not come?

He who gives life to the world
Him do I praise through the Guru's word.
His light is in all life born
Of the egg or womb or sweat or seed.
O Merciful Master, O Bounteous You
Grant me Your vision
That I may find salvation.

Nanak says: She who is in love with the Lord
Is infused with grace.

Magh (January-February)

Magh punit bhai tirath antar jania

The Lord has entered my being.
I make pilgrimage within myself and am purified.
I met Him.
He found me good
And let me lose myself in Him.

'Beloved! If you find me fair
My pilgrimage is made,
I am cleansed.
More than the sacred waters of Ganga, Yamuna and
    Tribeni mingled at the Sangam;
More than the seven seas,
More than charity, almsgiving and prayer
Is the knowledge of Eternity that is the Lord.'

Nanak says: He who has worshipped the Great Giver
                of life
                    Has earned more merit than those who
                    bathe at the sixty and eight places of
                    pilgrimage.

Phalgun (February-March)

Phalgun man rehsi prem subhae

She whose heart is full of love
Is ever in full bloom.
Joy is hers for she has no love of self.
Only those who love You
Conquer love of self.
Come, Lord, and abide in me.

Many a garment did I wear,
The Master willed not and

His palace was barred to me.
When He wanted me, I went
With garlands and strings of jewels and raiment of
   finery.

Nanak says: A bride welcomed in the Master's mansion
                    Has found her true Love.

GURU ANGAD DEV (1504-1552)
There are sixty-two hymns by Guru Angad
in the *Adi Granth*.

Jo sir saune na nivai so sir deejai daar

Cut off the head, O Nanak,
That bows not to the Lord;
Burn the wretched flesh
That feels not the pain of separation.

* * *

Akhin bajhon vekhna bin kana sunana

To see without eyes,
Without ears, hear,
To walk without feet,
Without hands, work,
To speak without a tongue—
Thus living, yet detached from life.

O Nanak, if you follow the word of your Master
You shall surely meet Him.

* * *

Ihu jagu sachche ki hai kothari

All the world is His dwelling place; the True
   One among us resides.
Whom He wills He makes one with
   Himself, whom He wills He destroys;
By His will is one rid of illusion, by His will another
   ensnared.
And which one of us can know who shall receive his
   grace?
Says Nanak, he alone finds the Supreme
   Guru, whose mind He illumines.

GURU AMAR DAS (1479-1574)
There are 907 hymns by Guru Amar Das
in the *Adi Granth*.

Manmukh lok samjhayiai kadon samjhaya jae

If you preach to the wicked
Can you turn them from their wicked ways?
They will not mingle with the good however much
   you try
But will tread their own wayward paths
For such is their desert.

There are two ways:
Love of the Lord and love of gold.
By His ordinance alone one finds the right path.
The good conquer their sinfulness
And the touchstone of the Guru's word
Declares them pure.

It is with the mind we must battle,
With the mind we must come to terms
And with the mind make peace.
The mind gets what it wills
By the power of Truth and love of the word.

Drink deep of the nectar that is the Name
And let your deeds be righteous.

If your battles are not with your own mind
But with others
You will have wasted your life.

The wicked surrender to their wilful minds
Their ways are false, their reward evil.
The good win their battles over their minds
For they have their thoughts fixed on God.

Nanak says: The good through Truth attain salvation
The wicked escape not the cycle of birth
and death.

* * *

Maya kis no akhiai, kya maya karm kamae?

What is maya? What acts spring from it?
The snare of joy and sorrow in which our lives are
caught,
The thought of self that moves us to action.
Without the word there is no wisdom,
Nothing to tear apart maya's veil of illusion,
Nothing to exorcise the ego.
Without love you cannot be a devotee,
Without the word, you will find no rest.
It is the word alone that conquers self
And destroys illusion.

The pious receive the gift of the Name
By gentle ways and good conduct.

Without the Guru one cannot tell
The good from the bad.
Without goodness, prayer has no meaning.
If God is in the heart
He can be met face to face.
He comes as gently as comes sleep.

O Nanak, raise your voice in praise of the Guru
By His grace you shall attain salvation.

* * *

Kajal phul tambol ras

She put black in her eyes, flowers in her hair,
With betel leaves sweetened her breath and her lips
    stained;
But the Lord came not to her bed
All her adornments were in vain.

Woman and man who just live together, speak not of
    them as truly wed,
When in two bodies a single light burns, then are man
    and woman truly wed.

Without the fear of the Lord
One cannot be a true devotee

For one has no love of the Name.
Love is born on meeting the true Guru.
Fear and love together give the proper hue
They kill the hunger of the ego
And with His Name, body and soul imbue.
Body and Soul thus cleansed, made of beauty rare
Give to the Lord, the Destroyer of Evil.
Both fear and love to him the Lord does give
Who in this world do truthfully live.

* * *

Anandu bhaiya meri mayi

Mother, my heart is full of joy
For I have found my true guru;
I found the true guru following the gentle path of *sahaj*
My heart resounds with cries of felicitation
Jewel-like ragas and their families of fairy-like houris
Have come to sing hymns of praise;
They within whom Hari resides, divine hymns sing
Says Nanak, I have attained bliss because the true guru
    I did find.

* * *

Ae man meriya tun sadaa rahe Hari naale

My heart, ever abide with the Lord Hari
Abide with the Lord and forget all your misery;

Gathering you within Himself
He will sort out all your affairs.
In every way He is your master
Why then let Him out of your mind?
Says Nanak, my mind, forever with the Hari abide.

* * *

Sache sahiba kiya nahi dhari tere

Master true, what is it that is not in Your house?
There is everything there
Only those You choose to give find it.
Lord grant me the gift of ever singing Your praise
So Your name gets imprinted on my mind.
The hearts of those wherein dwells the name
Always resound with hymns of praise
Asks Nanak, true Lord what is there not found in Your
    house?

* * *

Sacha nam mera adharo

Name of the true Lord is my support
With the true name's help, I lost all my hungers
It gave me peace of mind, contentment and fulfilled
    all my desires
Forever may my life be sacrificed to the guru who is
    so great

Says Nanak, ye men of God, cherish his words
For the name of the true one is my mainstay.

* * *

Vaje panch sabad titu dhari sabhage

All five kinds of musical instruments
Play in the hearts of the blessed;
In their blessed homes plays celestial music
Where God has infused his magic and might.
And the five evils (lust, anger, greed, self-love and
    arrogance) are suppressed
And the fear of death is no more
Only those who were predestined
Attach themselves and the true name find.
Says Nanak, there is always happiness
Where uninterrupted divine music plays.

* * *

Kalao masaajni ki-aa sadaeai hirdai hi likh leho

Why need you pen and ink? Write upon your heart.
Dye yourself in the colour of the Lord, and you are his
    forever.
Pen and ink will not endure, nor even what was written.
O Nanak, love of the Lord shall not perish; it is a gift
    from the True One.

* * *

Anadu sunhu vadbhagiho

Hearing the divine music all your heart's desires will
    be fulfilled.
You will find the great creator,
All your worldly cares will disappear;
Pain, sickness, worry will vanish
When you hear the true hymns of praise.
Pious and holy men will be overjoyed, assures the true
    guru.

Purified are they who hear,
And purified they who sing
The Lord is to be found in his words.
Says Nanak, you clasp the sacred feet of the guru
And you will hear divine music for eternity.

GURU RAM DAS (1534-1581)
There are 679 hymns by Guru Ram Das in the *Adi Granth*.

Gur satgur ka jo sikh akhae

He who would call himself the disciple of the Guru,
   the True Guru,
Should rise early and meditate on Hari who is God.
He should bathe in the 'nectar-pool'
And labour during the day.
He should hear the words of the Guru his teacher
And repeat the names of Hari
For then will his sins be forgiven him and his suffering
   cease.
As the day advances, let him sing the hymns of the Guru
And keep the Lord in his mind in all he does.
He that repeats the name of Hari with every breath
And with every morsel that he eats
He is the real Sikh, him the Guru loves.
He to whom the Lord is gracious
Listens to the Guru's teaching and becomes his
   disciple.
Nanak, your servant begs for the dust of the feet of Sikhs
Who worship and lead others to the path of worship.

* * *

Mero sundar kaho milai kit gali?

What shall I do to meet my Love?
O you who worship Him show the way
Let me follow in your footsteps.
The path that leads to Him is of obedience to Love's
    commandments,
Of treasuring them in the heart.
They matter not: your untidy scattered locks,
Your short stature, your bent and ugly body.
If you find favour in His eyes
You shall be beautiful and sit beside Him.

Our Lord is the One Lord
And we his consorts.
She who His beloved is
Is the best of wives.

O Nanak, why need you bother yourself
If the Lord wills, He will show the way.

* * *

Har ke jan satgur satpurkha

We seekers of the Lord beseech you our true guru,
To you who is truth personified we pray;
We are but worms and vermin seeking your protection,

Be merciful, illumine our hearts with your name.

My friend and mentor, suffuse my heart with the name
　of Rama;
Let teachings of the guru my life sustain
Let singing praises of the Lord show me the way
And be my evensong.

Men of the Lord are fortune's favourites
They are ever firm in their faith
And ever thirst for the Lord.
Finding the elixir of the Lord's name
Their thirsts are slaked.
In the company of holy men
His virtues they praise.

Most unfortunate are those,
And caught in shackles of life and death,
Who have not tasted the nectar of His name.
Those who sought not the Lord's protection
Nor the holy congregation,
Are damned in this life and for lives to come.

Those devotees blessed with the guru's companionship,
Bear marks of blessed fate on their foreheads.
Twice blessed is that congregation
Where the nectar of the Lord's name is found.
There, says Nanak,

The Lord's name is illumined and enlightenment
found.

* * *

So purakh niranjan, hari purakh niranjan

Our Lord is without blemish, our Lord is untainted by
illusion
He is beyond comprehension, endless and beyond
reach;
All worship You, the real author of all creation;
All creatures are created by you, you are their provider
and giver;
O men of God, ponder over Him! He is the remover of
all sorrows;
He himself the Lord, and the servant,
Says Nanak, of what worth is a mere human?

You dwell in every body, flowing uninterrupted,
You are the only one in every one;
Some you endow with riches, others you reduce to
beggary,
It is all a part of your inscrutable design;
You are the giver,
You yourself the decider of how it is spent
I know not any other like you;
You are the infinite God, your expanse unknown,

How can I put your qualities in words?
Whoever serves you, on him will Nanak sacrifice his
   life.

Those who meditate on you, those who worship you,
Will live in peace for all their lives;
Those who meditate on you, will gain salvation
And be freed from the noose of Yama;
Those who worship the Lord who is without fear
They will themselves be freed of fear;
Those who serve the Lord
Will merge in the person of the Lord;
Twice blessed are they who contemplate God
Nanak will give his life for them.
The treasury of your worship is beyond count
Your worshippers worship you in infinite ways;
Worship you who are infinite and without end;
Many are the ways to worship you
Many forms of penance and endless the forms of
   prayer;
Many a sacred text is read,
Many a way to serve you, including the six Karmas;
Says your slave Nanak, those worshippers are best
Who please the Lord and by Him are blest.

You are the primal Lord, creator beyond reach
There is none equal to you;

From age to age you are the only one
Forever the only one who gives stability;
What pleases you comes to pass
What you do comes to be;
You created all that exists
You will take it all back as you will;
Your slave Nanak sings your praises
Who knows all that is worth knowing.

* * *

Toon karta sachiar mainda saeen

You are the true Creator, you are my Master
What pleases you will come to pass,
What you give, I receive.

All that exists belongs to you
You are worshipped for your creation;
To those you are pleased with,
You grant the jewel of your name.
Men of God find it, followers of Mammon lose it;
You abandon the wordly, clasp the godly to your
    bosom.

You are the mighty river, all within you is contained
Without you nothing exists;
All living creatures are your play things

Some get separated from you
Others by your grace merge in you.

Those you give the gift of wisdom do you appraise
And forever sing songs in your praise.
He who serves you, finds peace of mind
And in the Lord, he gently a place finds.

You are the Creator, you the executor
There is none besides you,
You create and keep everything in your sight.
Says your slave Nanak, for the godly you came to light.

GURU ARJAN DEV (1563-1606)
Guru Arjan's 2,218 hymns form the largest single
contribution in the *Adi Granth*.

Prit lagi tis sach sion marai na avai jae

I love Him who is the Truth.
He dies not; nor is reborn to die again.
I flee from Him but He does not forsake me,
He is in all our hearts.

He knows the sorrows of the poor,
He destroys their pain and suffering,
He upholds those who serve Him.

This wondrous form is the Formless One
The Guru took me to meet Him, O Mother.

Listen, my brothers, befriend Him
Shun the love that is maya's snare
For none that love maya are happy.

He knows all
He is the Great Giver
He is serene
He is charitable
He is the true friend and helper
He is very great

He towers above all
And is limitless.

He has no childhood, no old age
His Court and His Commandments are Eternal.
What we beg, He grants.
He is the hope of those without hope.

One vision of Him destroys all sin
And our soul and body find tranquility.
With single-mindedness mediatate on the One
And the mind's illusions will be dispelled.

He is the treasury of goodness
Ever youthful He is
And full of charity.
Worship Him all the time
Forget Him not night or day.

Those who are His chosen
Are befriended by Him.
I dedicate my body, soul, and my possessions,
And sacrifice my life to Him.

He sees and hears all
He dwells in the recesses of our hearts.
Even the ones who show Him no gratitude

Are helped by Him.
Nanak's God is ever forgiving.

* * *

Ja ko muskal at banai dhoi koi na dei

When troubles come and you have no one to turn to
When enemies are at your heels and your kinsmen
   desert you
When hope is fled, all hope shattered
Let your thoughts turn to Him who is your Maker
And no ill wind will harm you.

The Master is the strength of the feeble.
He does not come and go, He is forever where He is.
The Guru's words shall reveal the truth to you.

When you are weak and frail,
Without clothes, without food,
When no one drops a coin in your apron
Nor gives you comfort.
When no one helps you and you succeed not in your
   actions
Let your thoughts turn to Him who is your Maker
And your affairs will forever go well.

When cares crowd upon you
When your body is foul with disease

When you are obsessed with thoughts of your wife
    and your kinsmen
Are sometimes happy and sometimes sad,
When restless and agitated you wander in all directions
Without a moment's rest, without a moment's sleep
Let your thoughts turn to Him who is your Maker,
And your body and mind will forever be whole.

When lust, anger, and attachment have you captive
And full of greed you are ever wanting, covetous,
When you have committed the four sins
(Drunk wine, thieved, fornicated, and killed)
And in the company of devils have become a devil,
When neither books of wisdom nor songs nor hymns
    of praise
Fall upon your ears
Let your thoughts turn to Him who is your Maker
And in the twinkling of an eye will you be saved.

Books of wisdom you might know by heart, and recite
Prayers and practise the penances of the Yogis, all
    pilgrimages undertake
And twice perform the six good acts
(Learn and impart learning to others,
Sacrifice and make others give in sacrifice
Give alms and accept charity),
Bathe in holy water and do worship.

If you love not the Lord with all your being,
It is all in vain and for you there is nothing but hell.

Empires, kingdoms, and baronies may be yours
And the wherewithal of power and pleasure.
You may own orchards, beautiful and bountiful,
And have power over others without any limit
And indulge in sports and pastimes to keep yourself
    amused.
If your thoughts turn not to Him who is your Maker
Yours will be the rebirth as a serpent.

You may have much wealth,
Live well and have gentle ways
Love deep your mother and father, sons, brothers and
    friends,
Own armies of footmen and archers, and many to bow
    to you in salutation,
Many to shout 'Long may you live.'
If your thoughts turn not to Him who is your Maker
You shall surely be dragged down to hell.

Your body may be free of fever and without sores,
Your mind free of cares and affliction.
Without ever the thought of death
Night and day you may enjoy yourself
And take everything as your own
Without any reserve or hesitation.

If your thoughts turn not to Him who is your Maker
For you will be the servitude of hell's demons.

Those to whom the Creator is merciful
Is given the company of holy men,
The more they are with such companions
The more they love Him.
He is the Lord of good and evil
There is none other than Him.

O Nanak, only by His Grace will you find Him,
The True Guru, whose Name is Truth.

* * *

Tun per sakh teri phuli

You are the tree,
And the world its branches.
You were unknown
And You made Yourself manifest.
You are the ocean,
You the bubbles, You the foam;
There is nothing that is without You.
You are the string,
You the beads strung on it;
You the knot and the central bead of the rosary.
The beginning and the end and the middle
Are You; none else is there beside You.

You are *nirgun*, transcending all attributes,
You are *sargun*, teeming with attributes,
You are the Giver of all joy,
You are without desire
Yet the passionate colouring in all desire
You symbolize.
You alone know Your ways
You alone comprehend Yourself.

You are the Lord
You His servitor
You the secret, You its revelation.
Nanak, Your servant, shall ever sing of You
If You grant him a little grace.

* * *

Tun mera pita, tun hain mera mata.

You are my Father
You my Mother
You are my Kinsman
And my Brother.
Everywhere You are my Protector
What reason have I to harbour fear?

By Your grace I recognise You.
You are my Support
You are my Pride

I know of no other beside You.
The world is but an arena for Your sport.

You are the Creator of life and matter
The Dispenser of all destiny.
All that comes to pass is by Your decree;
We have no hand in the performance.

Those that have pondered on Your nature
Have found great bliss.
By singing Your praise
My heart has found peace and comfort.
O Nanak, the Almighty Guru Himself rejoices,
Since you have won the great battle.

* * *

Kin bidh kusal hot mere bhai

Tell me brother, how does one find peace?
How to find the God, Rama, who is our help?
Maya has spread its net everywhere to catch us.
There is no happiness in the home of the humble
Nor in the lofty mansions of the rich.
In false pursuits we waste our lives
We joy in the possession of horses and elephants
In armies and ministers and retinues of servants,
Thus do we put the halter round our necks
And fasten the noose of the 'I am.'

We wander in all directions seeking power
We sport in the company of damsels
And being beggars
Dream ourselves to be kings.
One truth has the True Guru told me
What the Lord does His followers should accept as
    the best.

Nanak, the servant, says: By killing thoughts of self
    and merging in Him
Is found peace, O brother of mine.
Only thus we find God who is Rama.

* * *

Anik jatan nahi hot chhut-kaara

It is not through trickery that one gets release
However many the tricks one tries.
Much learning only increases the load of sorrows.
It is only service and the love of God
That takes one with honour to His Court.
O Soul of mine! If you make the name of the Lord
    your shelter
No ill-wind shall harm you.

As the sight of a boat on stormy seas
As the light of a lamp in the dark
As the warmth of fire in winter's cold

Does prayer bring solace to the soul.

The thirst of your soul will be quenched
Your hopes fulfilled
Your mind will cease to wander
For nectar is the name of the Lord
And the friendship of godly men.
The healing balm of prayer is given only to him
To whom the Lord is gracious and grants the boon.
Those whose hearts echo the name of the Lord Hari
Their sorrow and pain, O Nanak, are banished.

* * *

Bhuj bal bir brahma sukh sagar

O Lord of Mighty Arms,
Creator of all things,
O Ocean of peace!
Take me by my hand and raise me
Who am fallen in a pit.

My ears hear not
My eyes have lost their light
I am crippled, afflicted
Like a leper I come stumbling to Your door
And cry for help.

You are the Lord of the fallen,
Above You there is no Lord
O Compassionate One,
You are my Companion, Friend, Father and Mother.
Let Nanak bear the imprint of Your feet in his heart.
Let Your saints ferry me across the fearful ocean
    of life.

* * *

Jeh man mai karat gumana

When man has pride in his heart
He wanders around like one possessed.
When he is like dust under the feet of others
He then knows that God is in every heart.
The reward of humility is knowledge of the gentle path
It is the gift the True Guru gave me.

When a man looks down upon others as lowly
He becomes full of fraud and deceit,
When he has no care of 'mine' and 'thine'
Then none bears him ill-will.

When he claims 'this is mine' and 'this too is mine,'
His troubles weigh heavy on him,
When he recognizes Him Who is his Creator
Then he is not burnt with envy.

When he is bound by bonds of desire
He comes and goes and is under the eyes of Yama,
When he has shaken off all delusion
God holds back no secrets from him.

If he keeps secrets from the Lord
Then for him is pain, suffering and punishment,
When he recognises Him as One, the Only One
He comprehends all he needs to know.

When he madly seeks wealth
He is neither satisfied nor is his craving lessened,
When he frees himself of such desires
Then Lakshmi, the lotus goddess of wealth, walks in
    his train.

If by His Grace he meets the True Guru
In the temple of his heart the lamp is lit,
When he is indifferent to victory and defeat
Then alone he knows the Truth.

He alone is the Doer, He alone makes us do
He has wisdom, thought and discretion
He is not far, He is not near
Yet He is with everyone.
Says Nanak, worship the Truth with all your heart.

* * *

Prithmai tyagi haumai rit

I discarded the love of self
And the ways of the world,
I gave up distinction between friend and foe
And was blessed with knowledge to recognise the
    godly.
In the cave of *sahaj* I sat in meditation
Saw the light, heard divine music
And pondered over the word in utter bliss.
I was the blessed bride taken by the Lord.
Nanak, your servant who has thought much about this,
    says:
He who listens and then acts
Lands safely on the other shore.
For him there is no more birth and death, no more
    coming and going.
With the Hari he is one forever.

* * *

Gun avgun mero kachu na bichario

My merits and demerits You did no reckon
Nor looked upon my face, complexion or adornment.
I knew no winsome ways nor manner of deportment
But You took me by the hand and drew me to Your bed.
Listen my friends—My Groom has become my Master

He puts his hand upon my forehead and calls me His
    own.
What know the foolish men of the world?
Now has my union been consummated
My Groom knows my sorrows and has dispelled them.
The moonlight shines in my courtyard
Night and day I live in ecstasy with my Love.
My raiments are redder than the rose
I glitter with jewels and garlands of flowers.
My Love looks at me and I have the wealth of the
    world.
I have no fear of the wicked demons.
I am eternally happy and full of joy—
I have found Truth in my home.

Says Nanak: She who has adorned herself for the Lord
                    Hers is the true consummation.

* * *

Jaise kirsan bovai kirsani

As a farmer sows his field
And mows it at his will
Be it green or ripe,
So does the Lord take at His will
All that is born
And dies.

Only the worshipper of Govind is immortal.
The day is followed by the night
The night passes and comes the dawn,
But the wretched sleep in maya's delusion,
Only the rare ones are roused
By the Grace of the Guru.
O Nanak, forever sing praise of the Lord
It cleanses the heart and illumines the face.

* * *

Jan tun sahib tan bhau keha

What fear have I when You are my Master,
Who else shall I worship?
If I have You I have everything,
I look to no other.
Lord, much venom have I seen in the world,
You are my Shepherd, my Protector,
Your Name is my comfort
You know the anguish in my heart
To whom shall I tell my sorrow?
Without Your Name the world is in turmoil,
Only those who take Your Name find peace.
What shall I say? Who will listen to me?
The Lord alone can speak.

You are the Maker.

Forever and ever You are my hope,
In making me great, You magnify Your greatness,
Now and always it is You I will worship.

Nanak's Lord is the constant Giver of Joy.
His Name is my only strength.

* * *

Subh chintan gobin raman, nirmal sadhu sang

O Lord, grant me these: purity of thought,
Will to worship, company of godly men,
And the power never to forget You for even a moment.

The night is damp with drops of dew
Stars twinkle in the sky,
Those beloved of the Lord are risen
For those the Lord loves are ever awake.
Night and day His Name is on their lips
In their hearts rest His lotus feet
Their thoughts never stray from Him.

Abandon pride and lust, they silt the mind
And smother it in the smoke of sorrow.
Nanak says, Those that love the Lord are ever awake.

* * *

Meri sejarye adambar baniya

Upon my bed I awaited His coming,
My heart leaped with joy when I heard His footsteps.
He came to me, He Who is my Lord and Master.
My desires were fulfilled, I was with joy replete.
He took me in His arms, limb to limb we lay
And my anguish was gone.
My life, my soul, my body were all refreshed.
My wishes were granted; I worshipped Him.
Blessed was the hour I met Him.
Says Nanak: I have met the Lord of Lakshmi
And joy all is mine.

My companions ask me, by what signs did I know He
    was my Master?
Filled with ecstasy, I could not utter a word in reply.
His goodness is profound and hidden.
Even books of wisdom know not His dimensions.
With love worship Him and meditate on His Name
And ever let your voice be raised in His praise.
Our Lord is with virtues replete, His knowledge is
    supreme and complete.

Says Nanak, she who is filled with His love
Goes gently to His bed to rest.

* * *

Nadi tarandri mainda khoj na khumbe

Deep the waters of the stream,
I cannot swim, my feet no foothold find.
I shall ferry across for I am full of love
On the Lord's feet is fixed my mind.
O Nanak, my love is the Boatman.

Only them will I call my friends
At whose sight evil thoughts disappear;
I have sought them over all the world,
O Nanak, such men are very rare.

Let the Master be in your thoughts,
His worshippers have seen Him.
Keep the company of godly men
Then shall your sorrows end, your heart be clean.

The saintly break the fetters
At their sight devils scatter and hide,
They make us fall in love with Him
By Whose Will we all abide.

High is His seat, the highest of all;
It is beyond reach, there is nothing beyond it.
Day and night your hands in prayer join
With every breath bring the Lord to mind.
If He be gracious, He shall grant us the company of
the godly.

* * *

Bar vidanre humas dhumas

Dense and terrifying is the forest,
Petrifying the stillness before the storm,
Screams of terror assail the wayfarers' ears.
You are our Leader; I hold tight the rope and follow
And thus, O Nanak, traverse the wild woodland.
Those in whose company our voices rise in prayer
Are verily our true companions.
O Nanak, shun the friendship of those
Who think of nothing but themselves.

That time is auspicious when we enter the presence of
    the True Guru
When we befriend the godly and sorrows do not assail us
When we find blessed rest and escape the cycle of
    birth and death;
For then we see the One Creator wherever we turn
    our gaze
We know the supreme wisdom of turning our thoughts
    on God
We know that the best speech is the words of prayer
We know His commandments and find joy in submission.
Such the Lord treasures, for such are of the true mint.

* * *

Bajigar jaise baji pae

As a performings juggler
Acts many parts, wears many disguises
And takes off his mask when the show is done
So is our Creator one, the only One.

What forms he brings into being
And then does banish?
From whence do they come
Where do they vanish?
Countless waves rise from the waters
Many an ornament is made from gold,
Whenever a seed is sown,
It ripens into many fruits, though the seed is one.

The same Light of Heaven is reflected in water
In a hundred pitchers contained,
The pitchers may burst
But the light remains.

Maya deludes, it creates greed and desire,
When freed of delusion we see
The Creator is One.
He is immortal, He does not die.
He did not come, He will not go.
I have met the Guru
He cleansed my mind of the ego.

Says Nanak: So was I saved
Thus did I achieve supreme salvation.

* * *

Umkio hio milan prabh tain

My heart leaped up to behold the Lord
I heard of His coming, in my heart made His cot,
I went out to meet my Beloved
I wandered everywhere but saw Him not.

O poor heart, how wilt thou get peace of mind?
I will give my life if the Lord I find.

One couch is spread for the Lord and wife.
She slumbers, Her Lord awaits ever awake
But like one drunk she sleeps.
If the Lord embrace her, she too will wake.

I am without hope, many days have passed
In many lands and continents did I seek Him.
I cannot live if I clasp not His blessed feet
If He be kind, my fortune will turn and we shall meet.

He was good and gave me the company of the true
And my restless wanderings did then cease.
In my house I found my Lord
All my adornments do Him please.

Says Nanak: The Guru has lifted illusion's veil.
        Whichever way I turn, O brother, I see
            my Lord
The doors of ignorance are thrown asunder
The restless mind has ceased to wander.

* * *

Ghar meh thakar nadar na avai

The Master is in the home, but we do not see Him
His image in stone round our necks we wear
Deluded by maya everywhere we wander
Churn water in hope of butter, kill ourselves with
The stone that we the Master call
That stone itself will be our fall.

Sinners we are, to our Master's salt untrue
We cannot cross in a boat that of stone is made.
Nanak met the Guru and then knew his Master
He prevades the earth, the sky and water.

* * *

Ek rup saglo pasara

He is One but does in all things pervade
He is the merchandise, His is the trade.
This truth only the rare ones learn

He is present whichever way we turn.

He has many hues, yet He is of one colour
He is the water and the wave
He is the temple and is the God therein
He is the priest, He is the prayer
He is the yogi, He is the Yoga.
The Lord of Nanak in all things you see
Yet the Lord is from all things free.

* * *

Mrit mandal jag sajiya

The world He created as a house of slaughter
Like castles of sand children make, it lasts not long
It rots as paper under the drip-drop of water.

See for yourself, in your mind weigh:
Yogis, men of action, and householders,
Have left their homes and belongings and gone
    their way.

As a dream at night, the world is such
And all you see must perish.
O Fool, why love you this world so much?

Open wide your eyes, see and learn:
Your friends and brothers in the shade are gone,

Some have left, others await their turn.
Only those who have served the Lord absolute
Find their places at Hari's gates
They stand firm (and will not be turned away).

Nanak is the servant of the Lord
O destroyer of Evil, protect him.

* * *

Prabh ji tun mere pran adhare

O Lord, You are the hope of my life,
You I greet, before You I prostrate myself
To You I offer salutations, to You I make sacrifice.

Seated or standing, in sleep or in waking
My thoughts ever turn to You.
My sorrows and joys, all that passes in my heart
I bring to You.

You are my support, my strength, my knowledge,
My wealth are You and all the kinsmen I have.
Says Nanak: What You do is for the best
He finds peace at the sight of Your feet.

* * *

Hamro subhao sada sad bhulan

It is in our nature ever to sin,
And in Yours to redeem us.

* * *

Kahe re man chitvahi udmu

Why dear heart are you worried about what to do
When the good Lord Himself provides sustenance for
   you.
Creatures among rocks and boulders He created,
Before them, their means of living He placed.

* * *

Mere madhao ji

Beloved Madhava! One who keeps company of saintly
   men is saved
By Your grace, above others he is placed;
As out of dead wood,
Green leaves sprout.

* * *

Janani pita lok sut banita

Mother, father, kinsmen or wife
None will abide with you all your life!

The Lord provides for all mankind
Why then harbour fear within your mind?

* * *

Ude udi aavey se kosa

As geese and swans fly hundred and hundreds of miles
Leaving their young behind!
Who feeds them? Who nurtures them?
They know and remember Him all the time.

* * *

Sabhi nidhan das asat sidhan

All nine treasures and eighteen occult powers
Are in the palms of our Lord and Master,
For Him, will Nanak sacrifice his life over and over
    again.
There is no end to your existence
Unmeasured forever will remain your domain.

* * *

Bhai parpati manukh dehuriya

You have been granted the human form
Now is the time to meet your Lord Govinda!

No other activity will be of any avail
In the company of the holy, sing praises of the name.

* * *

Saranjami lagu bhavjal taran kai

Prepare yourself to swim across the fearful life's ocean
Do not waste life by dabbling in colourful illusions.

* * *

Japu tapu sanjmu dharmu na kamaiya

We have not earned merit through prayer or penance
Nor exercised control over our minds;
Nor performed sacred duties assigned to us,
Neither have we served men of God;
We are lowly, says Nanak, our acts those of sinners,
We seek refuge in you, so save our honour.

* * *

Tera keeta jaato nahi

All that you have done for me is beyond my
    comprehension,
I am because of you.
Ignorant, bereft of all virtue,
Still you took mercy on me.

After the mercy, you showered divine grace,
Let me befriend the true guru
Says Nanak, His name gives me life,
My body and mind shall ever thrive.

* * *

MUNDAVAANI

Thaal vichi teeni vasute paiyo

On this platter you will find three things;
Truth, contentment and contemplation
Also the nectar of the name of the Lord
Which gives sustenance to life
He who imbibes and ingests it will be saved
No one can afford to give it up
Preserve it in your hearts forever and ever.
In the darkness spread over the world,
You will be saved by clasping the feet of the Lord
Says Nanak, for the whole expanse is the Lord's.

GURU TEGH BAHADUR (1621-1675)
In all, 115 hymns of the ninth Guru were
incorporated in the *Adi Granth* by his son and the
last Guru, Gobind Singh.

birtha kahon kaun sion man ki

Whom shall I tell of the anguish of my heart?
Greed has me in its hold.
I rush madly in the ten directions
Seeking gold.
I suffer much wanting life of ease
And serve all kinds of people,
And like a dog go from door to door
But I have no thought of prayer.
I waste my human existence,
I have no shame when people laugh at me.
O Nanak, why sing you not in praise of the Lord
And rid your mind and body of impure thoughts?

* * *

jo nar dukh mai dukh nahi manai

He who in adversity grieves not
He who is without fear
He who falls not in the snare of sensuality
Who has no greed for gold knowing it is like dust.
He who does not slander people when their backs are
    turned

Nor flatters them to their faces.
He who has neither gluttony in his heart
Nor vanity nor attachment with worldly things.
He whom nothing moves,
Neither good fortune nor ill,
Who cares not for the world's applause,
Nor its censure,
Who ignores every wishful fantasy
And accepts what comes his way as it comes.
He whom lust cannot lure
Nor anger command,
In such a one lives God Himself.
On such a man does the Guru's Grace descend,
For he knows the righteous path.
O Nanak, his soul mingles with the Lord
As water mingles with water.

* * *

Sadho eh tan mithiya jano

This body is a lie, O Seers,
The spirit of God within the only truth.
Why do you wallow in sweet illusions,
Why are you attached to worldly possessions
When nothing will go with thee?
Put away all thoughts of praise or blame,
And fix your mind on His glory.

In every heart dwells the Perfect One,
Says Nanak, know him as the Lord.

* * *

Sukh main bahu sangi bhaye

Many were my friends in the hour of happiness,
In sorrow none remains.
Says Nanak, recite the Lord's Name, O mind,
He alone is yours in the end.

* * *

Na hi gun na hi kachhu jap tap

I possess no virtue, nor merit of worship;
How shall I redeem myself?
Says Nanak, Thou art my only refuge,
Give me the boon of courage, O Lord.

* * *

Jagat bhikhari firat hai

All the world is a wandering beggar,
The Lord alone is the bestower.
Says Nanak, remember Him, O heart,
Then all your efforts bear fruit.

* * *

Bar bhiti banai rachi pachi

A wall raised of sand
Will not last four days;
So are the joys of maya:
Know this, O mind, and be free.

* * *

Bal chhutkiyo bandhan pare

I have no strength, I am in shackles,
All my efforts are in vain.
Says Nanak, now save me, Lord,
As you saved the elephant king.*

* * *

Bal hova bandhan chhute

My strength returns, I am unshackled,
All my efforts avail;
Says Nanak, it is all in Thy hands, Lord,
You alone can save.

*When Gajendra, the king of elephants, was attacked by a
    crocodile, he was saved by Vishnu.

GURU GOBIND SINGH (1666-1708)
Guru Gobind Singh added his father's compositions
in the *Adi Granth*, but none of his own. His writings
are collected in the *Dasam Granth*. Many of the last
Gurus' hymns are used in Sikh ritual and prayer,
especially the evening prayer, *Rehras*.

From Akaal Ustat:

As sparks flying out of a flame
Fall back on the fire from which they rise;
As dust rising from the earth
Falls back upon the same earth;
As waves beating upon the shingle
Recede, and in the ocean mingle
So from God come all things under the sun
And to God return when their race is done.

* * *

Mitter Piyare nun, haal mureedan da kehnan

Beloved Friend, beloved God, Thou must hear
Thy servant's plight: when thou art not near
The comforts' cloak is a pall of pest,
The home is like a serpent's nest;
The wine chokes like a hangman's noose,
The rim of the goblet is an assassin's knife.
With Thee shall I in adversity dwell,
Without Thee life in ease is life in hell.

* * *

Hamari karo hath dae rachcha

Extend Your hand, be my protector
Fulfil my mind's desire;
Your blessed feet be my mind's repose
Cherish me like a relation close.

* * *

Hamare dusat sabhae tum ghavhu

Of all my foes be the destroyer
Extend me Your hand, be my saviour;
Bless my family with everlasting peace
Creator, preserve my Sikhs and devotees.

* * *

Mo rachcha nij kar dae kariyae

Save me with Your own hands I pray
Slay all my enemies today;
Let all my wishes come true
Give me an unending thirst for worshipping You.

* * *

Tumhi chchadi koyi avar na dhiyaun

Make me meditate on none but you
Whatever I wish, I get from You;

Help my Sikhs and devotees cross life's ocean
Single out my enemies and slay them one by one.

* * *

Ap hath dae mujhae ubariyae

With Your own hands uplift me
From fear of death set me free;
Forever remain on my side
May Your sabre and banner by me abide.

* * *

Rakhi lehu muhi rakhanhare

Protect me O Great Protector
Lord of saints, helper of your loved ones;
Always friend of the poor, foe of the evil remain
Lord, the fourteen worlds are within your domain.

* * *

Kal payi brahma bapu dhara

When the right time came You created Brahma the
    creator
When the right time came You created Shiva the
    destroyer
At the right time, You sent Vishnu the preserver;
Eternal time is Your plaything forever.

* * *

Javan kal jogi siv kiyo

When you who made Shiva an ascetic, recluse,
And then Brahma vedic knowledge pursue:
To that moment, when You adorned the universe,
I render my salutation.

* * *

Javan kal sabh jagat banayo

He who did the entire world create
Also created gods, demons and yakshas;
He is the alpha and omega of time, the only incarnation
Understand that He is my only Guru.

* * *

Ghat ghat ke antar ki janat

The throbbing of every heart He hears
Pain of the good and wicked He knows;
From the tiny ant to the mighty elephant
He casts a benign look on all and is content.

* * *

Santan dukh paye te dukhi

When the godly suffer, He too suffers
When they are happy, He too rejoices;
The pain of those in pain He shares
The beating of every heart He hears.

* * *

Jab udakrakh kara kartara

In expansive mood the Creator did the world create
His creatures different shapes and forms did take;
Whenever He withdraws in Himself in a whim
All of them will merge in Him.

* * *

Nirankar Nribikar Nirlambh

Formless, immaculate, self-supporting
Primal, stainless, beyond time, self-born;
Only fools try to probe into His existence
Even sacred texts know not His essence.

* * *

Ekae rup anup sarupa

You are in many forms manifest
At one place You are a beggar, at another a king;
You create life from egg, womb and sweat

And from the earth many riches beget.

* * *

Kahun phul raja hae baetha

At some places You are a flower-bedecked king sitting
    on his throne
At others You are a hermit shrunken to the bone;
Your creation is a display of wonderment
You were before time, through the ages, self-existent.

* * *

Ab rachcha meri tum karo

Protect me now, to You I pray
Uplift my Sikhs, my enemies slay;
Wherever forces of evil, power wield
Crush the filthy lot in the battlefield.

* * *

Je asidhuj tav sarni pare

Those who come under Your flag and hegemony
Their wicked enemies die in terrible agony;
Those who fall at Your feet and seek protection
For all their hardships You find solutions.

* * *

Jo kali ko ik bar dhiyae hae

Those who to the timeless God but once do pray
Will never again see an evil day;
At all times He will be their protector
All evil-doers He will instantly scatter.

* * *

Ek bar jin tumae sambhara

Those who meditate on Him even once will see
From fear of the noose of death they are free;
A man who invokes Your name, Lord,
Is freed of misery, evil and pain.

* * *

Khadag ket mae tihari

In the battlefield Your protection I crave
Extend your hand and Your servant save;
In every place be my guide and helper
From wickedness and sorrow grant me shelter.

* * *

Panyi gahe jab te tumre

Ever since I clutched Your feet,
My eyes have not beheld another.

With Ram, Rahim, Puran and Koran and others I did
    not bother.
Of Simritis, Shastras, Vedas and other texts I took no
    notice.
It is by virtue of Your banner and Your sword,
What I have written is not mine but Your sacred word.

* * *

Sagal duar kau chchadi kae

I passed by all doors before I stopped at Yours
Hold me in Your arms, and my honour save
Gobind will forever be Your slave.

* * *

Dehra maseet soi puja au namaaz oi

He is in the temple as He is in the mosque,
He is in the Hindu worship as He is in the Muslim
    prayer.
Gods and demons who guard the treasures
Of the God of riches, the musicians celestial,
The Hindus and the Muslims—they are all one.
They have each the habits of different homes,
But all men have the same eyes, the same body,
The same form compounded of the same four
    elements—

Earth, air, fire and water.
Thus the Abhekh of the Hindus and the Allah of
   Muslims are one,
The Quran and the Puran praise the same Lord.
They are all of one form,
The one Lord made them all.

* * *

Kon bheo mundia sanyasi

One man by shaving his head
Hopes to become a holy monk,
Another sets up as a yogi
Or some other kind of ascetic.
Some call themselves Hindus
Others call themselves Mussalmans...
And yet man is of one race all over the world;
God as Creator, and God as Good
God in His Bounty and God in His Mercy
Is all One God. Even in our errors
We must not separate God from God!
Worship the One God,
For all men the One Divine Teacher.
All men have the same Form.
All men have the same Soul.

* * *

Naam thaam na jaat roop na rekh

He has no name, no dwelling-place, no caste;
He is the Primal Being, Gracious and Benign,
Unborn, Ever Perfect, and Eternal.
He is of no nation and wears no distinguishing garb;
He has no outer likeness; He is free from Desire.
To the east or the west,
Look where you may,
He pervades and prevails
As love and affection.